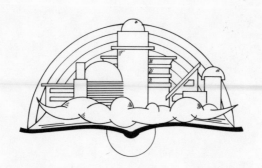

Inherited Wealth

Studies In Ephesians

Inherited Wealth
Studies In Ephesians

Tom Julien

BMH Books
Winona Lake, Indiana 46590

ISBN: 0-88469-034-2

COPYRIGHT 1976
BMH BOOKS
WINONA LAKE, INDIANA

Printed in U.S.A.

Cover design and artwork: Tim Kennedy

To Doris,

who has made Ephesians 5:25

a growing joy

Tom

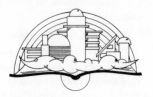

Preface

If you are studying Ephesians for the first time, I envy you.

From a prison in Rome Paul allows himself to be transported into the heavenlies; the result is the letter to the Ephesians, one of the truly great portions of the New Testament.

It is great in its depth. This is no new convert writing, but one who has invested all for Christ and knows Him as few others. It is great in scope. Within paragraphs we are swept from eternity to eternity and confronted with new dimensions in our conceptions of the universe and God's plan. After contemplating heavenly mysteries, we are immediately called back to responsible everyday living and healthy human relationships

And it is great in its theme, for here more than in any other letter Paul reveals the Church. The Church is a mystery—something hidden in ages past but now revealed. Above all, the Church is Christ's body, and it is glorious.

We talk a lot about churches. Our libraries are full of books that tell what churches ought to be like and how they ought to function. We pride ourselves on having the right kind of church government and are quick to defend the autonomy of the local congregation.

But the local church at its best can only be an imperfect expression of the true. It is perfected not by better programs, but by beholding the glory of the invisible. More than anything else in our churches, we need a new vision of the Church. Though Paul addresses his letters to local churches, his preoccupation is *the Church*, in its universal sense. If a local church succeeds in becoming fully autonomous, it ceases to be church, for particulars can find meaning only as they relate to universals. The local church which becomes an end in itself is on the road to spiritual self-destruction, even though it will continue to exist as an organization. And the same is true of denominations.

As you meditate on the pages of this remarkable document, Paul's letter to the Ephesians, do not be afraid to lay aside some of the pressing little concerns of local church life in order to gain a renewed vision of what the Church really is. Paul probably could not have written this kind of letter in the midst of his labor in Ephesus; God had to set him aside in a prison to give him the perspective necessary.

And unless you are willing to set aside some time for the study of this letter, you may miss the privilege of being caught up with Paul into the heavenlies.

It would be a pity, for that is where the real action begins.

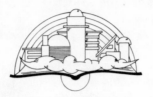

Table of Contents

1

God's Great Plan

EPHESIANS 1:1-14

THE CHAPTER OUTLINED:

I. **Blessed Be God**
   1. Paul states that God's blessings for us are spiritual
   2. Paul states that God has blessed us "in heavenly places"
   3. Paul states that God has blessed us "in Christ"

II. **Father, Son, and Spirit**
   1. Chosen by the Father
   2. Sealed by the Spirit
   3. Redeemed by Christ

III. **The Mystery of His Plan**
   1. God's plan is a mystery
   2. God's plan concerns the administration of the present age
   3. God's plan is that all things should be summed up in Christ
   4. God's plan concerns us

The letter to the Ephesians begins in a conventional way, much the same as any other letter written by anyone else in Paul's time. The author is the man who met Christ on the road to Damascus. Saul's heart is afire with hatred for a new sect—the followers of Jesus of Nazareth. God had other designs, and Saul the persecutor became Paul the Apostle, the greatest of all missionaries and the one to whom God revealed that the Church, instead of being a sect, was a central part of God's eternal plan.

Ephesus was the largest city in Asia Minor and the place where Paul had spent more than two continuous years of ministry. One has only to read the touching account of his farewell to the Ephesian elders in Acts 20:17-38 to realize that the bonds between him and the Ephesian Christians were strong.

Paul wrote from Rome around A.D. 61. He was in prison awaiting trial before Caesar for the accusations made by the Jews in Jerusalem. During this imprisonment Paul was visited by a fellow Christian named Tychicus. This visit provided the occasion for writing the Ephesian and Colossian letters plus the short epistle to Philemon.

But what follows the initial two verses of greeting in the Ephesian letter is far from conventional. In one sweeping paragraph, unique in his letters, the Apostle pours himself out in a display of praise that reaches from eternity past to eternity future and spills out into the heavenlies. Here we have a divinely inspired hymn of three stanzas, each addressed to one person of the Trinity and each ending in a doxology to God's glory.

I. BLESSED BE GOD (1:3)

Verse 3 is a call to worship. This remarkable verse uses the word "bless" in three ways: "Blessed be . . . God . . . who hath blessed us with all spiritual blessings."

We use many words with only a vague idea of their meaning, and such a word is "bless." How many times does it occur in your prayers? Have you ever stopped to define it?

In itself the word translated "bless" is very simple; it merely means "to speak well of." But when a simple word like "bless" comes in contact with the infinite God, it almost explodes. When man speaks well of God, this becomes worship, the noblest and most uplifting of human experiences. When God speaks well of man, His words are transformed into spiritual realities which become a part of His plan and which we can appropriate into our lives.

1. Paul states that God's blessings for us are spiritual. We often try to distinguish between material and spiritual blessings. We should not forget, however, that *all* God's blessings are spiritual, whether they concern our body or soul, because they all come through His Spirit. A blessing is anything that benefits us; a spiritual blessing is a benefit which is communicated from God's Spirit through ours.

Jesus once said that God is Spirit, and we must worship Him in spirit and in truth (John 4:24). This sounds a little vague at first, but when we understand that the spirit is the seat of consciousness, intelligence, and will, we see that we worship when we give ourselves to God in an intelligent and conscious way. Worship comes from the spirit, not the feelings, though feelings can help. Many things feel spiritual even though they are not. True spirituality is always conscious, intelligent, and expressed through the will.

In every generation the Church must be on guard against various forms of short-circuit spirituality—the kind that by-pass either the will, the consciousness, the intelligence, or all three. Recently a young man confided that though formerly his prayer life had been a chore, he had now entered into a new kind of experience that released the door of his inner man and allowed his words to flow profusely. The main problem is that now when he prays, he does not understand what he is saying. If prayer is not conscious communication, what is it? God can hear even when words come hard and we are in a bad mood, if these words bring our spirits in contact with His.

2. Paul states that God has blessed us "in heavenly places." This phrase occurs several times in the letter, and to grasp it we must accept the fact that the universe is more than what we see and feel. It exists in dimensions beyond our perception. Along with the visible world, with its time and space as we know it, there is an invisible world—or maybe even several invisible worlds. Our bodies are so constructed at present that they cannot enter into contact with the invisible world any more than an AM radio can receive FM waves. But the Scriptures indicate that the invisible is just as real as the visible, or even more real, and that in fact the visible could not exist at all were it not for the invisible.

Our spiritual blessings are in this invisible world, the heavenlies. Though our bodies cannot presently perceive the invisible, our spirits can, for they can escape the limitations of time and space and enter into the presence of God. This we do, in fact, every time we establish genuine spiritual contact with Him.

Our part is to bring these blessings from the invisible world to the visible. Because God has blessed us in the heavenlies, we must willingly *appropriate* our blessings so that they can become realities in our experience. God has blessed; our part is to keep open the doors of communication and trust between us (that is what faith is), so that heavenly blessings can be translated into our world of time and space.

3. Paul states that God has blessed us "in Christ." The hymn of praise is addressed to the Father, Son, and Holy Spirit, but it is permeated throughout with Jesus Christ. Read it through to see how many times His name occurs. And rightfully so, for anything coming from God to man must pass through Him. He is the *Word* of God, and has been for all eternity. He is the *man* Christ Jesus, the unique mediator between the infinite and the finite.

Some seek blessings and miss Christ. Others seek Him and find both.

II. FATHER, SON, AND SPIRIT (1:4-14)

Christ is our means of contact with God; He is the way to the Father. Through Christ we have access to God in His fullness: God who is Trinity. Paul is not concerned with trying to prove how one God can exist in three persons. This former Pharisee who recited from youth, "Hear, O Israel: the Lord our God is one Lord," has almost met Christ face to face and has experienced the Holy Spirit's power in his life. For him the Trinity is not a doctrine to be argued but three persons whom he knows and adores indiscriminately.

And his worship is a gem of perfection. To praise God the Father, Paul goes back into eternity past before the world began. To praise the Holy Spirit, he goes into eternity future and our great heritage. But when he praises God the Son, the present cannot contain him, and he breaks out of the narrow confines of time and space to reveal God's great plan of reconciling all things in Christ.

1. Chosen by the Father (vv. 4-6).

God chose us before creating the world. Many people are bothered by a negative self-image, the result of unfavorable judgments or comparisons. If you are tempted to feel you are worthless, go with Paul back to the beginning of things. Even being chosen by men for something brings satisfaction, for one of man's basic desires is to feel needed. But to be chosen by God, to have been known personally by Him and desired by Him even before the world began—this makes our worth eternal.

Why did God choose some and not others? It is a question which has bothered many, and one which we cannot fully answer. After all, He did the choosing, not we, and He had reasons. Elsewhere Paul indicates that the choice was based on foreknowledge, implying that we were completed persons in the mind of God before creation, and that there was something about us that made God choose some and not others, even though that something had nothing to do with merit or superiority. One thing is sure: God chose only those who were willing to be chosen. God had to see this willingness in us before we were even made. And even though we may never fully understand why He chose us, we can still worship Him for it.

Further, we are clearly told of His purpose in choosing: that we might be holy and blameless. "Holy" means being completely consecrated to God; "blameless" means to be without fault. Through Christ, God has justified us, declaring us blameless in His sight. Through the Spirit, God is sanctifying us, bringing us into the reality of holiness. We are destined to be perfect. It is quite obvious that if God's goal for us is holiness, we ought to be well on the road toward that goal right now, reminding ourselves, as does Paul, that God is accomplishing His purpose in love.

God predestined us to be adopted into His family. Whom God chooses, He predestines. The word should not frighten us; to predestine simply means to establish in advance. Predestination is the guarantee that the choice God made before the beginning of the world will be fulfilled. He does not leave things to chance. Chance could destroy man's freedom; loving predestination does not. Only in a world which God controls can He guarantee man the privilege of getting what he really wants, what God knew he wanted before beginning it all.

We are predestined to be adopted. For the Romans, the practice of adoption concerned their own children; adoption was a ceremony which conferred the right of inheritance. This practice provided the background of Paul's thinking concerning divine adoption: by adoption God confers upon His children their inheritance. All this is accomplished according to the good pleasure of His will.

When we begin praising God for our election and predestination, we begin to see that God's glorious Church, though historically born on the day of Pentecost, has been in the mind of the Father for eternity. It is a part of His choice, guaranteed by His person, according to His will.

2. Sealed by the Spirit (vv. 13-14). From the beginning of the hymn of praise and eternity past, we are making a huge leap to the end of the hymn, which leads into eternity future. This passage is something like a mountain; whether you start from the beginning or end, you are caught up toward the summit, where in the middle of his hymn of praise Paul breaks out into eternity present, into the heavenlies where our distinctions of past, present, and future lose their meaning.

We have already noted that God's blessings in eternity have to be appropriated by man in time and space—in other words, in everyday living. Our inheritance is the result of our being chosen and predestined in the mind of God. But it is also the result of hearing and believing the word of truth, the good news of our salvation, as Paul clearly states in verse 13. Those who have been chosen by God are those who hear and believe the Gospel; those who hear and believe the Gospel are those who have been chosen. Whether you approach it from heaven or earth, from time or eternity, the result is the same.

What a tragedy that some have been so bothered about predestination that they have refused to believe the good news of salvation! Our part is clearly defined: we are simply to listen to the Word and to trust it; when we do, the Holy Spirit becomes our "seal" and our "earnest," guaranteeing our inheritance forever. And the Holy Spirit is God just as are the Father and the Son. For this we bless Him just as much as for the knowledge that He chose us in eternity past.

Seals are not so common as they were in the past, but all of us have seen ancient documents bearing a bit of wax imprinted with an official signet ring. There are many kinds of seals, but they nearly always denote ownership and protection. God puts His seal upon us because we are no longer our own; we belong to Him. Because we belong to Him, He pledges himself and all His resources as a guarantee that this ownership will be respected. It is no wonder that people have trouble believing in the security of the believer if they look at it only from man's side. But from the eternal viewpoint, what a difference! How can life or death or anything else separate from God those whom He has both chosen and sealed with His own person?

He is also the "earnest" of our inheritance. This old English word simply means down payment. God himself, in the person of the Holy Spirit, is the down payment of our eternal inheritance; the rest will be paid in due time.

3. Redeemed by Christ (v. 7). Blessed be the Father who has chosen us in eternity past; blessed be the Holy Spirit who seals us for eternity future. And blessed be Jesus Christ, in whom we *have* redemption.

The middle of Paul's hymn of praise focuses on the present and centers on Christ. We are redeemed by Christ, and in Him we have the remission of our sins.

The term "redemption" refers to the liberating of someone in captivity. In the classic use of this term, redemption always implied payment of a price. One still sees in the main squares of some southern towns the auction block where once slaves were sold. Had a rich benefactor come to town the day of the auction, he could have freed them by paying their price.

It seems paradoxical that God should have to redeem those whom He had already chosen as His own. Yet, though God chose men, mankind rejected God, and this rejection brought man into a slavery for which no human redemption was possible—the slavery to sin and death. The price God had to pay was horribly high: we are only redeemed by His blood. Anyone who fails to see the direct relationship between the forgiveness of his sins and the death of Jesus on the cross has entirely missed the message of the Gospel. There was no other way. Jesus' death was the only possible answer to the divine dilemma: how a holy God could share His eternal love with a defiled humanity.

Through redemption we have forgiveness. The word used here means much more than simple pardon. It is the word "remission," which means that God took our sins from us and placed them elsewhere—on Christ Himself. They are not simply covered over; they are gone, as far as the east is from the west.

III. THE MYSTERY OF HIS PLAN (1:8-12)

Now Paul's hymn of praise bursts out, climaxing in an exalted vision of God's great plan. How necessary for us, so completely submerged in our world's machinery, distorted values, and conflicting philosophies, to break through the clouds of confusion in order to see what the world is all about! What is God trying to do? What is our purpose in life? Here we are transported beyond the veil of the immediate into God's very mind and presented with an all-encompassing statement of His purpose for present human history. Because God chose us before the foundation of the world, because He redeemed us with His blood, because we are sealed with His Spirit, we have a part in His plan, and that part is intimately tied to His Church, "the fulness of him that filleth all in all."

1. God's plan is a mystery (vv. 8-9). In the sense in which the word is used in Paul's writings, a mystery is not something mysterious or hard to understand. It is something that cannot be known unless it is revealed, something formerly hidden but now made known. God's plan is something that He "purposed in himself," "according to his good pleasure." Human history is simply the unveiling of something that has existed already in the mind of the Creator. Paul has no place for a world of chance or hazard.

But though man through wisdom cannot discover God's will, spiritual wisdom is necessary to understand it. God's grace has abounded toward us "in all wisdom and prudence." The first term seems to indicate the insight necessary for understanding divine truth, whereas the second refers more to the application of that truth. Spiritual insight is a gift of God for which we have the right to pray (James 1:5-6).

In other words, there is only one way to know what God is doing in this world and what He wants us to do. It is to listen to Him. Since the plan originated in God's mind, only He can reveal it.

2. God's plan concerns the administration of the present age (v. 10). The word translated "dispensation" means literally the management of a household. Much has been learned in recent years about the principles of good management. Where there is good management, each person in an organization has the opportunity to discover his gifts and use them fully. In our times of discouragement let us remind ourselves that God is still the ultimate manager of the universe, even though Satan has usurped power that is not rightfully his. Though we are faced with a world that seems to be going haywire, and though we are deeply puzzled by its injustices, we must seize by faith the truth that in the "fulness of times"—this present period of history which God is filling with His Spirit—God is managing according to a plan. His household includes both heaven and earth, the seen and the unseen.

3. God's plan is that all things should be summed up in Christ (v. 10). Just before Jesus went back to heaven, He declared, "All power is given unto me in heaven and in earth." The word there for power is *authority.* What then is God's plan? It is to bring *all things,* both in heaven and in earth, under the authority of Jesus Christ. He is the great focal point of the universe. He is the summary of human history. It is God's will "that in all things he might have the preeminence" (Col. 1:18).

The scope of God's plan is all-encompassing: all things everywhere.

This means all men. Of course, all men will not willingly accept Christ as their King, but we are nevertheless told that someday every knee will bow before Him and confess Him Lord, many to their eternal shame.

"All things" means all knowledge. Though the godless philosophies of men seem at times to threaten the very foundations of truth, truth will nevertheless prevail, for Christ is the truth. Some day every imagination and thought will be brought to obedience to Him (II Cor. 10:5).

"All things" even means the principalities and powers of the spiritual world. For Christ is "far above all principality, and power, and might, and dominion, and every name that is named, not only in this world, but also in that which is to come" (Eph. 1:21).

To be sure, much more than the Church is included in this great statement of God's plan. As we continue to read Ephesians, however, we shall discover that at the heart of God's plan is the Church, for it is Christ's body and fullness, through which He has chosen to reveal Himself in this present world.

4. God's plan concerns us (v. 11). It is a mistake to identify the inheritance mentioned in verse 11 with that of verse 14. Verse 14 promises an eternal inheritance. But the inheritance of verse 11 is present: it is an inheritance in the plan that God is accomplishing right now in His universe. What Paul is saying is that in God's management, we have been given a job, and this job is according to the predestination of Him who works all things according to the counsel of His own will. God's plan includes no unemployment.

What is our job? It is given to each according to his gifts and capacities. But though diverse, our tasks must reflect God's basic purpose. Certainly it is vain to attempt to seek God's will for our lives without going back to the final instructions Jesus gave His followers. Remember, He said all authority was given Him in heaven and earth. But He said more: "Go ye therefore, and teach [make disciples of] all nations, baptizing them in the name of the Father, and of the Son, and of the Holy Ghost: teaching them to observe all things whatsoever I have commanded you: and, lo, I am with you alway, even unto the end of the world" (Matt. 28:19-20).

Sooner or later every thinking Christian must face the question, "How can my life have the most influence for God in this world?" We have seen many let their vision of God's call become blurred by the crying needs of the immediate. But His plan is clear: to bring all things under the authority of Christ. His method is plain: to turn men into disciples.

To find our place in His plan is to praise Him, not just by words, but also by life. It is to allow our lives to be lived in the same way as Paul ends each stanza of his hymn of blessing: "that we should be to the praise of his glory."

Questions for Discussion

1. What is a "spiritual" blessing? How does it differ from other blessings? How do we receive spiritual blessings?

2. Paul frequently uses the term "the heavenlies." What does he mean by the term? In what way can we be in contact with the heavenlies?

3. In a predestined world is man really free to believe or disbelieve? How can we reconcile God's election with man's free choice?

4. What is God's eternal plan, and what is our part in it?

5. What is the Holy Spirit's ministry to the believer?

2

His Body

EPHESIANS 1:15-23

THE CHAPTER OUTLINED:

  I. Paul and Prayer
     1. Paul's prayers reveal his deep concern for the churches
     2. Paul prays without ceasing
     3. Paul's prayers begin with thanksgiving
     4. Paul's prayers were spiritual

 II. Spiritual Vision
     1. That you might have
     2. That you might know

III. The Exaltation of Christ
     1. God demonstrated His power in raising Christ from the dead
     2. God demonstrated His power in setting Christ at His right hand
     3. God demonstrated His power in putting all things under Christ's feet
     4. God demonstrated His power in making Christ the Head of the Church

The major theme of Ephesians is the Church. In Paul's hymn of praise in 1:3-14 we were caught up into the heavenlies, where we saw that God's plan is to bring together all things under the authority of Christ. The letter to the Ephesians will show us that the Church occupies a central place in this plan.

Now, in verse 15, we return abruptly from the heavenlies to the earth, and to the church at Ephesus. Though Paul writes about the glory of the universal Church, he never forgets that he is writing to local churches and to real people. His spirit can soar to celestial heights, but his feet remain planted firmly upon the earth. This wonderful balance is one of the marks of Paul's greatness and is seen throughout his writings. For instance, immediately after his superb presentation of the resurrection in I Corinthians 15, he states, almost without pause, "Now concerning the collection . . ."

It is by prayer that Paul can go from the heavenlies to Ephesus without even leaving his prison cell. The Ephesian letter contains two great prayers: here, and in chapter 3. This one is a prayer for knowledge; the other is for love. Here Paul prays that we may be able to know the power that God manifested in Christ; in chapter 3 he prays that we may experience this power.

I. PAUL AND PRAYER (1:15-19)

Perhaps nowhere else do we learn so much about the Apostle Paul as in his prayers. If we had nothing more than these in our New Testament, we could begin to understand why God chose this man to perform the most significant ministry in the Church's history.

1. Paul's prayers reveal his deep concern for the churches (v. 15). The Apostle did not sever contact with his churches when he left them. He was concerned that they go on to perfection. "What is our hope, or joy, or crown of rejoicing?" he wrote to the church of Thessalonica. "Are not even ye in the presence of our Lord Jesus Christ at his coming?" (I Thess. 2:19).

Imagine, then, his joy when he heard about the faith of the Ephesian Christians, and their love for all the saints. These two terms, faith and love, seem to summarize the totality of Christian experience. Through faith we grasp the revelation of God's plan; through love we express it.

2. Paul prays without ceasing (v. 16). Many Christians are troubled by the command to pray without ceasing (I Thess. 5:17). They think that this means the Christian must pray all the time, and so they turn prayer into some kind of a vague perpetual God-consciousness, which it is not. Prayer is communication with God; communication requires thought. No one can pray constantly.

In fact, when we begin to read Paul's prayers carefully, we find that he claims to pray without ceasing for several different churches. Does this mean that all those churches were in his thoughts simultaneously? Of course not. What it does mean is that Paul did not cease to pray for churches after he left them. To pray without ceasing means to pray without quitting. Generally we have a strong urge to pray for something during a few days, and then we forget. Paul realized that if his churches needed prayer yesterday, they still need it today and will continue to need it in the days to come.

Because Paul prayed without ceasing for so many different churches, it is almost certain that he had some kind of system in his prayer life. To be sure, prayer was spontaneous for him; it crops out everywhere. But it was also systematic and organized.

3. Paul's prayers begin with thanksgiving (v. 16). Almost in the same breath that Paul said, "Pray without ceasing," he also said, "In every thing give thanks" (I Thess. 5:18). His prayers are an application of this principle.

It would seem that Paul had the habit of giving thanks before asking. He evidently forced himself to think of something positive about his converts before going into problems. A good example is the church at Corinth, where some really grave problems were present. Before attacking these problems, the Apostle stated, "I thank my God always on your behalf" (I Cor. 1:4).

To thank God for someone before criticizing him is to see the person from an entirely different perspective.

4. Paul's prayers were spiritual (v. 17). How many times do you pray for fellow Christians who (1) are in good health and (2) are not having financial problems? We often pray for other things; yet is it not true that too many of our prayers have a materialistic ring to them? God does want us to pray for people who have lost their jobs and are in the hospital; we have already pointed out that *all* God's blessings are spiritual blessings, whether they are for the body or the soul.

Yet, are you not impressed by the fact that Paul's prayers are of a different kind from most of ours? How many times have we asked that God give our brethren a spirit of wisdom and revelation . . . that He open the eyes of their hearts to the hope of His calling, to the riches of His inheritance, and to the greatness of His power?

The Apostle's prayers reveal a great man of God, a man who knew what it was to seek first the kingdom of God and His righteousness (Matt. 6:33), a man whose meat was to do God's will and to finish His work (John 4:34).

II. SPIRITUAL VISION (1:17-19)

Let us turn from prayer in general to this particular prayer. Paul's prayer for the Ephesians is essentially that they may have the spiritual insight necessary to grasp the truths God has revealed about His plan.

The heart of the prayer is the little phrase at the end of verse 17, "in the knowledge of him." The Christian faith is in its essence knowing God. In another letter Paul writes, "That I may know him, and the power of his resurrection, and the fellowship of his sufferings" (Phil. 3:10). We grow in the faith to the extent that we know Him. This knowledge of God, however, is not simply theoretical. Many people know a lot about God without knowing Him. The word used here for knowledge denotes a knowing by personal experience. To know God is to receive Him into our lives.

In Paul's prayer we have first a main request, then three secondary ones. Paul prays first that we may have the spirit of wisdom and revelation in our knowledge of God. Then, the eyes of our heart being enlightened, he prays that we may know three aspects of God's blessings. These aspects correspond roughly to the three parts of Paul's great hymn of praise in the first part of the chapter.

1. That you might have (v. 17). Paul's prayer is addressed to the God of our Lord Jesus Christ, for it is through Christ that God gives us His blessings. This God is called the Father of glory, a term which sums up all the transcendence of His personality. Paul is asking great things from God, and he uses great terms to address Him.

Paul never seemed to be very far from God. Throughout his writings, prayer and praise burst out spontaneously. However, though the Apostle was intimately familiar with his Maker, he never stooped to familiarity. He realized that the one to whom he prayed was the Almighty Creator, and that he was merely a sinful creature who could dare come only through the merits of Jesus Christ. This vertical relationship is also seen in Ephesians 3:14, where he says, "I bow my knees unto the Father of our Lord Jesus Christ."

The Apostle's request for the Ephesian Christians is that God will give them the spirit of wisdom and revelation in His knowledge.

In verses 8 and 9 we saw that God made known to us the mystery of His will through all "wisdom and prudence." Wisdom means insight into spiritual things, and prudence, the right use of this insight. Because wisdom and prudence were used to reveal God's truth, a spirit of wisdom and revelation is necessary to perceive God's truth.

When Paul in verse 17 speaks of the spirit of wisdom and understanding, it is impossible to know whether he is referring to God's Spirit or to man's. Some would say that the term has reference to both, that Paul is saying that man's spirit must be indwelt and moved by the Spirit of God in order for him to receive God's knowledge. Whether or not this is the exact meaning of the verse, the statement is true, for in another letter Paul states, "Eye hath not seen, nor ear heard, neither have entered into the heart of man, the things which God hath prepared for them that love him. But God hath revealed them unto us by his Spirit" (I Cor. 2:9-10). Man's spirit unaided by God's cannot grasp God's wisdom.

Paul is praying, therefore, that the spirits of the Ephesian Christians may be in tune with God's. He is praying that through the action of the Holy Spirit on their intelligence they will have spiritual insight into God's revelation and the ability to grasp what God is doing in the universe. Paul is praying that they will subject their thinking to divine revelation rather than to their own imaginations.

2. That you might know (vv. 18-19). The word "understanding" in verse 18 is changed to "heart" in later translations. When we receive the spirit of wisdom and revelation, the eyes of our heart are enlightened.

For the ancients, the heart was not simply the seat of the emotions; it was the innermost part of man, the place where knowledge resides and decisions are made. King Solomon said, ages ago, "Keep thy heart with all diligence; for out of it are the issues of life" (Prov. 4:23). To love God with all our heart is not merely to have a sentimental feeling toward God; it is to choose Him above all others.

Just as we need good eyesight to know what is going on around us in the physical world, so must we have good spiritual eyesight to know about our spiritual environment. And just as light is necessary for our eyes to function properly, the light that comes from the spirit of wisdom and revelation is necessary for the eyes of our heart.

Some people can walk through a forest in the spring without seeing the beauty of the flowers or hearing the song of the birds. This is a shame. But an even greater shame is the Christian who can walk through his spiritual experience without knowing what is happening in and around him because the eyes of his heart are not enlightened.

When the eyes of our heart are functioning, we can *know*. Paul prays for spiritual knowledge in three areas.

"That ye may know what is the hope of his calling" (v. 18). Here we are referred back to verse 4, which says we were chosen in Him before the foundation of the world. In order for the Christian to have correct spiritual vision, he must be able to peer clear back into eternity past and to see himself as being chosen by God for a purpose. Further, in order to function properly as a part of Christ's body, he must be able to look at his brother in Christ and realize that he also has been called and that he, too, is a part of God's plan. Many of our problems are the result of spiritual nearsightedness. We see only the immediate, and it is often not very pretty.

But when we are able and willing to take that long look back, then the present assumes hope, for if God chooses, He chooses for a purpose. "Being confident of this very thing," says Paul, "that he which hath begun a good work in you will perform it until the day of Jesus Christ" (Phil. 1:6).

"And what the riches of the glory of his inheritance in the saints" (v. 18). Here we are referred to verse 14, which describes the Holy Spirit as the down payment of our inheritance until the time in eternity future when all that God purchased in Christ will finally be redeemed. Therefore, correct spiritual vision with the eyes of our heart will let us perceive the future as well as the past. We must see the end of things as well as the beginning.

Paul knew by experience what it was to take the long look into the future when the going became difficult. He said, "We look not at the things which are seen, but at the things which are not seen: for the things which are seen are temporal; but the things which are not seen are eternal" (II Cor. 4:18). When things go wrong in the local church, we must be able to look out into the future to that glorious Church, "not having spot, or wrinkle, or any such thing." Correct vision comes not from getting up close, but from backing off until we can see the present in the perspective of eternity.

"And what is the exceeding greatness of his power to us-ward who believe" (v. 19). Here we are referred back to verse 13, which says that when we believed, we were sealed with the Holy Spirit. To redeem us, God had to use His power. And because we are believers, God endows us with power. Correct spiritual vision means not only looking into eternity past to see that we have been chosen, not only looking into eternity future to see that we have a glorious inheritance; it means also looking at the present to see that God's power is available to us.

Before Jesus went back into heaven, He told His disciples, "Ye shall receive power, after that the Holy Ghost is come upon you" (Acts 1:8).

What is power? It is the ability to act in accordance with one's nature and desires. God's power enables Him to perform His will and guarantee His plan, in spite of His enemies. God's power in us is His ability to act in us according to His will.

Paul prays that believers may know the exceeding greatness of this power. He literally heaps up words to emphasize the spiritual resources we have in God. In verse 19 alone four different terms are used in the original text to denote power, each one adding force to the Apostle's statement. We are not called to live the Christian life in our own strength.

Yet, why is it that when we believers face problems, we usually fail to draw upon God's power? Why is it that the Christian rarely reacts differently to conflicts from someone who does not know Christ? Is it because we forget that we are different, or is it because we choose to handle things our way instead of His? The Holy Spirit is in us, and His resources are available, but as Paul points out later in this letter, He can be grieved.

The next time we are faced with temptation, the next time we find ourselves implicated in a serious problem involving human relationships, the next time we seek to share the Gospel with someone, may the eyes of our hearts be open to His Spirit, so that we may know the exceeding greatness of His power in us.

III. THE EXALTATION OF CHRIST (1:20-23)

Paul's statements about power turn his thoughts from the Ephesian believers back to the heavenlies where this power has its source. The power at work in believers is the same power that God used in raising and exalting Jesus Christ after His death.

In these four verses we have the spiritual summit of the Ephesian letter: the exaltation of Jesus Christ far above all other power in heaven or in earth, in this age or the next. And it is here that Paul states the major theme of the letter: Christ, the head of the Church, which is His body.

1. God demonstrated His power in raising Christ from the dead (v. 20).
Others had been raised from the dead, but their resurrections were merely
reanimations. Their risen bodies were no different from those they possessed before dying. Our Lord, however, was raised to be the second
Adam. He was raised to be a life-giving spirit, in order to vanquish death
forever. "O death, where is thy sting? O grave, where is thy victory? The
sting of death is sin; and the strength of sin is the law. But thanks be to
God, which giveth us the victory through our Lord Jesus Christ" (I Cor.
15:55-57).

We can only wonder what kind of spiritual battles were fought over the
resurrection of Jesus Christ. Even when Michael the archangel sought the
body of Moses, perhaps to present him with the Lord on the Mount of
Transfiguration, he could not oppose Satan directly, but had to call on the
intervention of the Lord (Jude 9). Because of spiritual laws that we cannot
fully understand, Satan had power over death through the sin of the first
Adam. The Resurrection brought to an eternal end this power, reversing
the whole order of things. Christ became the firstfruits of the resurrection
of all who will someday live in Him. "As in Adam all die, even so in Christ
shall all be made alive" (I Cor. 15:22).

**2. God demonstrated His power in setting Christ at His right hand (vv.
20-21).** The "right hand of God" is the place of authority. Our Lord is not
standing in the presence of the Father serving, but seated, indicating His
lordship. He is ruling, and His rule extends not only over the earth, but
over the entire universe.

Though Jesus took the form of a servant and became obedient to death,
God "hath highly exalted him, and given him a name which is above every
name" (Phil. 2:9). The divine glory which Jesus willingly laid aside has
been restored; all authority in heaven and earth is His.

God has placed Christ "far above all principality, and power, and might,
and dominion, and every name that is named." This embraces all distinctions, titles, and powers of the spiritual world. Throughout the Bible, from
Genesis to Revelation, we are given glimpses behind the veil into the
invisible and are made to understand that the real battles are in the heavenlies. These are the powers against which we still must wrestle. But their
authority has been crushed, so that the weakest Christian, acting in
Christ's power, can resist the devil with the assurance that Satan will flee
from him.

Our Lord is already King of kings and Lord of lords, and one day the
great final act of God's plan, dramatically portrayed in the last book of the

Bible, will begin, when the "kingdoms of this world are become the kingdoms of our Lord, and of his Christ; and he shall reign for ever and ever" (Rev. 11:15).

3. God demonstrated His power in putting all things under Christ's feet (v. 22). Not only has Christ been put over all other powers, but also all other powers have been placed under His feet. At first sight this seems just another way of saying the same thing. But it is more. Not only is Christ given authority over all; all are forced to yield to His authority. Human rulers have authority over their subjects, but not all subjects obey this authority. When we read that God has put all things under Christ's feet, we must understand that this is a demonstration of God's power in directly and forcefully subjecting all things to Him.

The sin of the first man was not that he wanted to be free, for he already had his freedom. His sin was that he wanted to be autonomous, independent of God's authority. This is the essence of all sin. In Christ's rule there will be no autonomy. All things have been spiritually subjected to Him, and one day He will exercise His authority in fact, "that at the name of Jesus every knee should bow, of things in heaven, and things in earth, and things under the earth; and that every tongue should confess that Jesus Christ is Lord, to the glory of God the Father" (Phil. 2:10-11).

4. God demonstrated His power in making Christ the Head of the Church (vv. 22-23). One of the strange paradoxes among Christians is people who seem to be fascinated by Jesus Christ but who at the same time reject the Church. Either they know nothing about the real Christ, or they know nothing about the real Church, or both.

To be sure, most of those who seemingly reject the Church have had some bad experiences in local churches. Local churches do not always reflect the glory of the invisible Church. But every authentic local church is, in spite of its imperfections, a part of Christ's body in a special way.

The word "church" literally means an assembly of called-out ones. The Church is composed of all those who have been chosen and called by God in eternity past, who believe and are redeemed from Satan's dominion in the present, and who are sealed by the Holy Spirit for their inheritance in the future. When we say universal or invisible Church, we are speaking of all who have been called in every age; when we speak of the local or visible church, we mean the assemblies of Christians uniting in a particular time and at a particular place.

Christ is the head of the Church. In an organized body the head is the one who directs. In the physical body directions and the instructions originate in the head. In the spiritual realm Christ is the head of the Church; therefore, He issues the directions and orders to His Body.

The Church is Christ's body. In the letter to the Ephesians the Church is designated by several images, each supplying a facet of truth. The Church is a building, "fitly formed together." The Church is a bride, being prepared for union with Christ. And the Church is a body, through which Christ expresses himself, with each member playing a distinct part.

Yet in these verses it would seem that the word "body" is used as more than an image and that in a real way the Church is the spiritual body of Christ. For Paul goes on to say that the Church is the "fulness of him that filleth all in all." All of God that can be communicated to man will be revealed in the Church.

Imagine it if you can: He who has been exalted above all principalities and powers has chosen to express His fullness in the Church! This has to mean that the Church, too, is exalted above all other things, "to the intent that now unto the principalities and powers in heavenly places might be known by the church the manifold wisdom of God, according to the eternal purpose which he purposed in Christ Jesus our Lord" (Eph. 3:10-11).

Questions for Discussion

1. What does it mean to pray without ceasing? What are ways we can organize our prayers in order to pray more consistently?

2. What is the practical value of thanking God for others? How does this practice change our relationship with them?

3. What is meant by the "eyes of the heart"? In what way does the Holy Spirit enlighten them?

4. What do we mean by the power of God, and how can we see this power operate in our lives?

5. If Christ is seated above all principalities and powers, why is there evil in the world?

6. How do you think the Church represents the fullness of Christ?

3

New Men

EPHESIANS 2:1-10

THE CHAPTER OUTLINED:

I. We Were Dead
1. We were dead in trespasses and sins
2. We were in bondage to the world, the flesh, and the devil

II. We Have Been Made Alive
1. What God is
2. What God did
3. Why God made us alive

III. Saved By Grace
1. Salvation is by grace
2. Salvation is through faith
3. Salvation is a gift of God
4. Salvation is not of works

God demonstrated His power by raising Christ from the dead and seating Him in power at His right hand. Jesus Christ was named head of the Church, which is His body and which is destined to be the expression of His fullness.

Now, after only a fleeting glimpse of Christ on the throne, we are plunged abruptly to Satan's dominion and presented a graphic portrayal of spiritual death and bondage. The contrast between chapters 1 and 2 is startling and must have been even more so for the first-century readers, who had no chapter divisions.

Though the contrast is great, however, the connection is logical. Now that Christ is seated in the heavenlies, there is work to do upon the earth. He must build His Church. The Church is not an institution; it is His body, composed of men and women who without exception have two things in common: they have been dead in trespasses and sins, and they have been made alive in Christ.

For the individual, the Church of Jesus Christ starts right in these verses, for they are the classic New Testament passage on salvation by grace; no one is in the Church of Jesus Christ who has not passed through the experience depicted here. Through this clear presentation countless thousands have finally understood that salvation is a free gift from God. It cannot be merited; it can only be received.

I. WE WERE DEAD (2:1-3)

Many artists have depicted physical death, but the picture painted here by Paul is more dreadful than any of theirs. For this is a picture of spiritual death. Here the dead walk, engage in a way of life, and actively fulfill the desires of their sinful nature.

When God created the first man, He forbade him to eat of the tree of knowledge, saying, "In the day that thou eatest thereof thy shalt surely die" (Gen. 2:17). Adam disobeyed and ate, but the Genesis record indicates that he lived to be over 900 years old before his body was finally laid in a tomb. However, in the spiritual sense Adam *did* die the moment he sinned, for there are two kinds of death—death which concerns our bodies, and death which concerns our relationship with God.

The essential idea in death is separation. When one dies, he does not cease to exist; rather, there is a disintegration or separation of the elements which formerly constituted life. Physical death is the separation of the spirit from the body. Spiritual death is the separation of man from God, and since God is the source of life, spiritual death leads to complete disintegration.

1. We were dead in trespasses and sins (v. 1). The words "hath he quickened" are not in the original text. Perhaps the translators wanted to soften the impact of Paul's words: yet, his statement is blunt: we were dead. Apart from Christ the dead have no hope. Dead men cannot be healed or reformed. They can only be raised.

Physical death can have many different immediate causes—accidents, sickness, violence, or what we generally call old age. There is but one cause for spiritual death: sin. Paul uses two words to describe it. The first, "trespasses," refers to deviating from the right path. The second, "sin," refers to missing the mark. "The wages of sin is death" (Rom. 6:23).

In his letter to the Romans Paul tells how death entered the human race. Adam's sin brought death not only to him, but also to all humanity, for spiritual death is hereditary. "As by one man sin entered into the world, and death by sin; and so death passed upon all men" (Rom. 5:12). But though it is interesting to know how death entered the human race, we should remember that each individual is dead from his own transgressions and sins. Though we inherited death from Adam, we merited it by our own sins; we were individually and personally guilty before God.

2. We were in bondage to the world, the flesh, and the devil (vv. 2-3). The spiritually dead are totally unresponsive to God, but they are not unresponsive to other influences. They are very much alive to the world, the flesh, and the devil. They walk, live, and seek fulfillment. But they are spiritual corpses. Their feverish activity is not life; it is only bondage to forces that are bent on their destruction.

We walked according to the course of this world (v. 2). This verse literally says that we formerly walked according to the "age of this world." There is a present age belonging to this world, and there is a future age belonging to the world to come. The same idea occurs in Romans 12:2, where we are warned not to allow ourselves to be conformed to the present age, but to be transformed by the spiritual renewing of our minds.

Because the term "world" is used in several different ways, many people have difficulty understanding its meaning in passages such as this. In fact, many Christians, even while knowing that they are not to love the world or the things in it, have never come to a clear definition of the kind of world they are to avoid. They find it easy to identify certain worldly practices, but because of hazy thinking about the world itself they sometimes fall into either a spiritual isolationism or the sanctification of a value system which is thoroughly worldly even though given a coat of spirituality.

By "world" Paul means a system whose values are opposed to those of the Spirit of God. This value system is rather easily recognized by some of its basic characteristics. (1) It puts man before God. The world says, "Not Thy will, but mine, be done." (2) It puts self before others. Its emphasis is on using others, not serving them. (3) It puts the material before the spiritual. Those things that appeal to the senses take preeminence. (4) It puts the immediate before the lasting and the eternal. The world is furious if it has to wait for something.

But the world can be easily recognized only by those who have been torn from it and brought into a new kind of life. For those who are enslaved to its system, it has a way of creating the illusion that the spiritually dead are very much alive and that their kind of life is the only kind that really matters.

We walked according to the prince of the power of the air (v. 2). Though the expression "power of the air" is somewhat unusual, there can be no doubt as to the identity of the prince; it is Satan himself.

It comes as a surprise to some that Satan is a prince, but he is. He is the prince over an unholy hierarchy of spiritual powers. He is also the prince of this present world. When man sinned, Satan usurped what God had destined for humanity, dominion over the earth. At the time of the temptation Jesus did not dispute Satan's claim to the earth. Satan promised to give Jesus all the kingdoms of the earth in return for His adoration. But Satan's power has been broken, and when the Lord returns, the kingdoms of the earth will become His by divine right.

When we walk according to this present age, we are also walking according to its prince, for Satan is the unseen force behind the world and its values. To choose the world is to choose its prince, even without knowing he exists.

And here is the sinister note about walking according to the world. Its bondage is not simply in its power to captivate man's appetites and ambitions; this in itself is bad enough. But there is more. The prince of this world is also the spirit which is at work in the children of disobedience. While the world exercises its power of attraction from without, Satan, through the countless unclean spirits which are at his bidding, works from within. These spirits prey on the spiritually dead, pushing them to ultimate destruction.

We lived according to the lusts of our flesh (v. 3). The word "conversation" in verse 3 is an old English term for "manner of life." When we were spiritually dead, our life style was determined by our sinful nature.

The sinful nature is related to spiritual death in much the same way that physical sickness is related to physical death. Both are forms of disintegration. Paul calls the sinful nature "flesh," not because it is related to our material flesh, but because it so often shows itself in the carnal appetites.

In terms of modern psychology, the "flesh" would probably be located somewhere in the subconscious part of man, the part that becomes the depository of all his impressions, thoughts, and experiences when they drift out of his conscious thinking. It is the part of man which is beyond the reach of the will, the part where evil and good become hopelessly jumbled together with no moral guidelines, prey on the bodily appetites, then bubble up into the consciousness to trip and entice. When man lost contact with God, he also lost contact with part of himself. This unconscious part of man is like a hidden monster in the soul, growing more and more powerful until it totally enslaves the will.

The way of the flesh leads always downward. This is seen in Paul's revelation of sinful man in Romans 1:18-32, where we are carried lower and lower into the depths of depravity. And it is also seen in these verses in Ephesians.

First, the spiritually dead are characterized as simply living in the lusts of the flesh. This is depravity on the level of the instincts. Second, they are said to fulfill the desires of the flesh and the mind. The word "desires" has to do with the will; the word "mind" has to do with the consciousness. Though depravity is first instinctive, it eventually leads to enslaving the will and the mind. Third, the spiritually dead are by nature the children of wrath. This is the final and ultimate step, when act has become habit, habit a way of life, this way of life a consistent and true portrayal of one's nature.

Man's final destiny is to become thoroughly consistent with his true nature: thoroughly good, or thoroughly bad.

II. WE HAVE BEEN MADE ALIVE (2:4-8)

We were spiritually dead, headed on the downward path toward total depravity, egged on by the combined forces of the world, the flesh, and the devil. Only one power could arrest us—God.

Just as abruptly as Paul confronted us with the spiritual deadness of mankind, he now confronts us with divine intervention. This is exactly what Paul intends when he says, "But God . . ." Man in his deadness has no power to reach across that infinite chasm between his sinfulness and God's holiness. God had to take the initiative.

1. What God is (vv. 4-5).

God is rich in mercy (v. 4). The word "rich" carries the idea of fullness, of abundance. Because David, in Psalm 23, could say, "Surely goodness and mercy shall follow me all the days of my life," he could also exclaim, "My cup runneth over" (vv. 5-6). God's mercy is like a spring which never runs dry; the greater the need, the greater the supply.

In the Bible we often find the terms "mercy" and "grace" used together. "The Lord is merciful and gracious," says Psalm 103:8. And when Paul mentions the word "mercy," he can hardly wait to talk about God's grace, interjecting it in verse 5 before it logically comes into the development of his thought.

Both terms, "mercy" and "grace," refer to the unmerited favor of God to the sinner. In a way, you cannot talk about one without the other, for mercy refers to God's favor toward man in *withholding* the punishment he deserved, whereas grace refers to God's favor toward man in *according* the blessings he did not deserve. Salvation is not only escaping death; it is also receiving life and all that this life entails.

God is great in love (vv. 4-5). If the word "rich" carried the idea of fullness, the word "great" carries the idea of depth. The reason God's mercy can overflow like a spring is that its source is deep and unfailing. Mercy flows from love, and God *is* love.

The word used to designate God's love in the New Testament, *agape,* was almost unknown to the ancients, for this kind of love is not natural to man. *Agape* love flows from the subject to the object; it is not produced because of the object. God loves man not because He needs man, nor because of man's attractiveness, but because God *is* love in depth, and because God *chooses* to express His love to man.

It is only this kind of love that can bring God's grace to us, because, as we are reminded in verse 5, we are "dead in sins." Our sin is ultimately directed against God, the source of life, cutting us off from any spiritual union with our Creator. Our sin has brought us spiritual defilement, has made us repugnant in God's eyes. But though we rejected Him, He did not reject us. Because He is love, *agape* love, He loves us in our sins, looking beyond our defilement and seeing our eternal worth.

"But God commandeth [proves] his love toward us, in that, while we were yet sinners, Christ died for us" (Rom. 5:8).

2. What God did (vv. 5-6). There can be no contradiction between God's person and His works; because God is rich in mercy and great in love, He must act, and His acts are worthy of His greatness.

God made us alive (v. 5). The word "quickened" means literally "made alive with." Spiritual death is separation from God; its only remedy is spiritual life: union with God. Spiritual life is the invasion of man by the Holy Spirit. It is regeneration, which means new birth. Man, who is dead in sin, will find life not through simply trying to please God or being faithful in religious practices. Corpses can be made beautiful, but they are still dead. "Except a man be born again, he cannot see the kingdom of God" (John 3:3).

God has raised us up together with Christ (v. 6). God not only gave Christ back the spiritual life He sacrificed on the cross; He also raised Him from the tomb. Because Christ has been raised, we have been raised with Him. It seems strange to see in passages such as this that the resurrection is presented as something that has already taken place for the Christian. To be sure, the resurrection of our bodies is yet future, but in a spiritual sense, we have already been raised. Spiritual resurrection means that our spirits have been liberated from the control of the flesh, reversing the disintegration produced by death. Paul develops this idea more fully in Romans 6, where he says, "Like as Christ was raised up from the dead by the glory of the Father, even so we also should walk in newness of life" (v. 4). The result is that the sinful nature need no longer reign in our mortal bodies.

God has made us sit with Christ in the heavenlies (v. 6). Among the many amazing things in this letter to the Ephesians, this is one of the most startling. Paul actually states that in some real way we are sitting with Christ, reigning, in the heavenlies. (Refresh your mind by rereading 1:20-23.) Though the thought staggers us, we must accept by faith that if Christ has been given authority over all the universe, in some way, spiritually, we share His authority.

Perhaps we can get a little glimmer of the meaning of this statement by realizing that Christ's elevation ended the spiritual authority of Satan and his unholy hierarchy. Being seated with Christ means receiving His authority over Satan in our own experience. Spiritually dead men are in bondage both to Satan and to the flesh. Spiritually living men are given authority both over the flesh, through our resurrection with Christ, and over Satan, through our being seated with Christ in the heavenlies.

But we must claim this authority. As Paul mentioned in chapter 1, God has blessed us in heavenly places; our part is to appropriate these blessings and translate them into the world of time and space, the world where we live.

3. Why God made us alive (v. 7). Paul not only reveals who God is and what He has done for man; he also gives us one of the central reasons for our salvation: that God might show the riches of His grace through all eternity.

The word "show" means something that appeals to the senses, something visible or tangible. Though we cannot now visualize the eternal state, there will be something to visualize. In concrete ways God will, for all eternity, put forth proofs of the surpassing riches of His grace.

The idea of eternity frightens many people. Imagine—living forever and ever! When you begin to think about it, it brings a feeling of uneasiness, almost anxiety.

In fact, the only thing that makes the concept of eternity tolerable is the concept of God's infinity. Without infinity, eternity would become hopelessly boring or even horribly so. Yet, God and his actions stretch continually beyond our capacity to comprehend—even in a world without end. God's infinity will make our eternity an experience of exciting discovery. Each new discovery will bring fulfillment. But there will always be more. And these discoveries will be directly related to God's grace.

III. SAVED BY GRACE (2:8-10)

Verses 8 to 10 contain one of the clearest statements of salvation in the entire Bible. If anyone can read these words and still think he must earn God's favor, we can only conclude that he is too proud to accept God's way. Paul summarizes salvation in four simple but mighty statements.

1. Salvation is by grace. The salvation Paul is speaking of is full and complete; it means bringing life to dead men, causing them to rise in triumph over their sinful natures, and seating them in power over spiritual forces. Lesser salvation *might* be possible for man to achieve through his own efforts or merits. But Biblical salvation can find its source only in God's freely bestowed favor on guilty and hopeless mankind.

2. Salvation is through faith. Faith is the channel through which God's salvation reaches man. Faith is man's response to God's grace. The word "faith" carries with it the idea of receiving (John 1:12) as well as believing. True saving faith involves the whole man: mind, emotions, and will.

Modern man has a tendency to turn faith into something irrational, making it a sort of intellectual leap into the dark. Some people pretend to have faith in the living Christ while rejecting what the New Testament says about Jesus and His death on the cross. This is nonsense. We can have faith, or confidence, only in what we can believe intellectually. Faith starts in the mind.

But of course faith must go further than the mind; it must reach the heart, where decisions are made. Once we really know the truth about Christ and salvation, we cannot remain neutral. We must either accept or reject. To accept is to receive Christ into our lives not simply as someone who lived twenty centuries ago, but as our personal Saviour and the Lord of our life.

3. Salvation is a gift of God. "The wages of sin is death, but the gift of God is eternal life" (Rom. 6:23). Some people read this verse as if faith is a gift of God, relieving man of any real responsibility in the act of believing. God's gift to man, through Jesus Christ, is salvation. A gift cannot be earned; it can only be freely accepted.

4. Salvation is not of works. The word "works" in 2:8 refers to something done with the express purpose of meriting or earning something. The better we do our "works," the more satisfaction we have in ourselves. But works are worthless with respect to gaining salvation. God does not want us to have satisfaction in ourselves; this destructive introspection is exactly what He is saving us from. He wants us to turn our eyes upon Him, so that He can liberate us for the realization of our eternal destiny. Boasting is out of the question.

However, though we are not saved by works, we are certainly saved for works, as Paul points out in verse 10. Faith without works is dead. We ourselves are God's workmanship; He comes to dwell in us in order to remake what sin sought to destroy. Further, we are created in order to create. In delivering us from bondage and giving us life, God unlooses our capacity for creativity. He is at work on us and in us. Good works are a part of God's plan for our lives, for "God hath before ordained that we should walk in them."

The good works that are a result of His working in us do not lead to boasting, but only to joy and a sense of worth. Fruit trees do not have life because they bear fruit; they bear fruit because they have life, fruit which is a source of blessing to all who partake. You cannot bring life to a dead apple tree by tying apples on it. But when you see apples, you know that there is life. And you do not praise the tree; you praise God who is the source of all good things.

What a contrast in ten short verses! From being dead in sins we have been saved and transformed into instruments through which God is at work to bring blessing. But we are more than simple instruments. We are Christ's Church. He works in us not simply as isolated individuals, but also as diverse members of His body.

As we continue to read the letter to the Ephesians, the veil covering the mystery of Christ's body will be drawn back further.

Questions for Discussion

1. What does the term "spiritual death" refer to? What is the relationship between spiritual death and the sinful nature?

2. Is it possible to live in the world without becoming enslaved by the world? Explain.

3. How can the spiritual truth of our being raised with Christ be applied to everyday living?

4. Why does the idea of grace occupy such a large place in the letter to the Ephesians?

5. How do you reconcile the apparent contradiction between Paul's insistence on grace and James's insistence on works?

4

A Holy Temple

EPHESIANS 2:11-22

THE CHAPTER OUTLINED:

I. **In Time Past**
   1. They were Gentiles in the flesh
   2. They were called uncircumcision
   3. They were lost

II. **In Christ Jesus**
   1. In Christ Jesus the wall of partition has been broken down
   2. In Christ Jesus the enmity has been abolished
   3. In Christ Jesus all are reconciled to God
   4. In Christ Jesus we all have access to God

III. **Now Therefore**
   1. We are members of a new society
   2. We have been built on the foundation of the apostles and prophets
   3. We become a building
   4. We grow into the temple of God

In reading the Ephesian letter you have perhaps noticed Paul's use of the pronouns "ye" and "we." In the first chapter he says, "We have obtained an inheritance," but a few phrases later makes a change, stating "Ye also trusted." The same distinction is made in chapter 2, where we read, "Ye walked according to the course of this world," then, "among whom also we all had our conversation in times past."

This distinction is not overly important in the verses we have just quoted. But in Ephesians 2:11-22 it emphasizes the most sensitive problem the Apostle had to face in evangelism and founding local churches, the relationship between the Jewish and Gentile Christians. By "we" Paul means his own race, the Jews, "who are Israelites; to whom pertaineth the adoption, and the glory, and the covenants, and the giving of the law, and the service of God, and the promises; whose are the fathers, and of whom as concerning the flesh Christ came" (Rom. 9:4-5).

But "ye" refers to the Gentiles, those who are "without Christ, being aliens from the commonwealth of Israel, and strangers from the covenants of promise, having no hope, and without God in the world" (Eph. 2:12).

Though this problem—the relationship of the Jewish and Gentile Christians—seems far from us today, we must attempt to understand its importance in the Early Church. Salvation came through the Jews. The Church born on the day of Pentecost was a Jewish church. Only when Paul began his great missionary trips did Gentile people accept Christ in great numbers.

Would Gentile Christians be expected to pass through the Old Testament in order to come to Christ? Could uncircumcised pagans sit side by side with Jews at the love feast? Would there have to be two churches, one for the Jews and one for the Gentiles?

This problem provoked the first church council, caused tension between Peter and Paul, perhaps led to the defection of John Mark on the first missionary journey, was the source of the first heresies, and was the indirect cause of Paul's arrest in Jerusalem.

It was absolutely necessary that Paul, before talking about the unity of the Church, attack head-on its greatest threat to unity. This he does in a wonderful way. Rather than requiring Gentiles to become Jews, or Jews to sacrifice their convictions, says Paul, God raises both to a new level of citizenship in a new body. All men, regardless of their past, are to become *new* men in Jesus Christ, their peace. Salvation means not only new life, but also new identity in a new household of faith. Old distinctions become meaningless.

In the first part of chapter 2 Paul said that in Christ we become new men morally and spiritually. Here he says that in Christ we become new men religiously and culturally.

This is a lesson that many Christians have yet to learn. For though we no longer have the Jewish problem, other cultural problems threaten the unity of many churches. If we are willing to let our vision of the Church be unclouded by personal prejudice, we shall see that churches can become places where all men, regardless of race, religious background, or culture, become fellow citizens in the community of faith.

I. IN TIME PAST (2:11-12)

The passage we are studying breaks down essentially into the same outline as verses 1 to 10. In both cases Paul shows what his readers were without Christ; then, what God did in Christ; and finally, what they have become in Christ. In verses 1 to 10 the subject is regeneration. Through God's grace the dead are made alive in Christ. In verses 11 to 22, the subject is reconciliation. Both Gentile and Jew are brought together into the same body through Christ our peace.

What characterized the Ephesians before they accepted Christ?

1. They were Gentiles in the flesh (v. 11). The word for Gentiles was "nations." The Jewish vision of the world was uncomplicated; people were simply divided between Jews and non-Jews.

Today there is much discussion of the question, "Who is a Jew?" Is one Jewish by race, religion, or citizenship? In Paul's day a Jew was one who could trace his ancestry back through the Patriarchs to Abraham. "We be Abraham's seed, and were never in bondage to any man," was the Pharisees' proud reaction to Jesus (John 8:33).

Therefore, the word "flesh" when applied to the Gentiles is used to designate race, rather than the sinful nature (as in verse 3) or the body (as in the latter part of verse 11). By birth Gentiles were cut off from the covenant promises given to Abraham.

2. They were called Uncircumcision (v. 11). When God called Abraham and gave him the promise of blessing, He established the rite of circumcision as an outward sign to mark those who were inheritors of the promise. Those who were circumcised showed by this sign that they were claiming their rights as Abraham's spiritual descendants. So important did circumcision become in Jewish thinking that the early Jewish Christians tried to impose this practice on Gentiles who received Christ.

Being uncircumcised, the Gentiles were cut off from God's promise both by birth and by religion.

3. They were lost (v. 12). The picture Paul paints of the Gentile world is just as bleak as that of the spiritually dead in verses 1 to 3.

They were without Christ. All of Jewish hope would find its fulfillment in the coming of the Messiah, the One who would rule eternally on David's throne. The word "Christ" is the translation of the word "Messiah." Through Him, blessing would come to humanity. Yet, the Gentiles had no messianic hope; they were without Christ.

They were aliens from the commonwealth of Israel. The commonwealth of Israel was the society over which the Messiah would rule and through which He would pour out His blessings. To be alienated from this commonwealth was to be cut off from the sphere of God's favor.

They were strangers from the covenants of promise. The word for stranger is "foreigner." Just as a nation accords its privileges to those who are its own citizens, even to the extent of protecting them when they are in a foreign land, so God's covenant promises were reserved for the true citizens of the commonwealth.

They were without hope. Hope without an objective basis is but an illusion. The Jews could have hope because their hope was rooted in something real—God's intervention in history. They could look back and see the way God called Abraham, the way He dealt with the prophets, the way He established the testament, and the way He led His people out of Egypt and gave them the Law. The Gentiles could find nothing similar in their histories; their religions were merely philosophical.

They were without God. The word translated "without God" is "atheist." This does not mean, however, that the Gentiles had no intellectual belief in God. As a matter of fact, their imaginations knew few bounds when it came to religion, and their gods were plentiful. Yet, their gods were merely the products of their own imagination. The real atheist is not simply one who refuses to believe; it is anyone who lives without the One who is the Author of all things and who has revealed himself to mankind.

When Paul says that the Gentiles were without God, he leaves no basis of hope for those who would like to believe that all religions lead to God if their followers are sincere.

II. IN CHRIST JESUS (2:13-18).

The contrast between verses 12 and 13 is as great as between verses 3 and 4. In both cases Paul paints a hopeless picture of man separated from God, a picture so hopeless that only divine intervention can help. In the first part of the chapter we found that God intervened to bring life to those who were spiritually dead. In this passage God's intervention reconciles those who are far from God and those who are near.

1. In Christ Jesus the wall of partition has been broken down (vv. 13-14). In the Temple complex at Jerusalem was a wall which separated the Gentiles from the Jews. Any Gentile going beyond that wall risked death. That wall symbolized the real spiritual separation between Jew and Gentile.

Moreover, the wall in the Temple prevented Gentiles from going into the place where sacrifices were made. They were denied access to the altar, where the blood of animals permitted reconciliation between God and man.

However, many years before the Roman soldiers would storm the city and raze the Temple, Jesus Christ was crucified, not merely outside the wall of partition, but outside the walls of the city itself. By His blood those who were far off and forbidden to participate in the animal sacrifices of the Temple were brought near. Through His death Jesus destroyed the spiritual wall between Jew and Gentile and, in fact, all barriers that might exist between men of any kind.

By shedding His blood, Jesus *became* our peace, making one those who were formerly divided. Bloodshed rarely produces genuine peace, but His was a death caused neither by His hatred nor by His greed. In dying for us, Jesus proved His love.

2. In Christ Jesus the enmity has been abolished (v. 15). Not only were Gentiles divided from Jews by the wall of partition which kept the Gentiles from the altar; they were also divided by the enmity provoked by "the law of commandments contained in ordinances." The Jews were the inheritors of the Law, and a zealous Jew would rather have died than give up one jot or tittle of the ordinances given him through Moses. The relation of the Gentiles to the Law would remain a point of contention both in the Church and without for years after the Gospel was preached to all men.

However, Jesus abolished this enmity in His flesh. By coming and living as a man, He established His righteousness; by dying for man He took upon himself man's sin, "blotting out the handwriting of ordinances that was against us, which was contrary to us, and took it out of the way, nailing it to his cross" (Col. 2:14). Jesus did not abolish the Law in dying on the cross; He fulfilled it, completing it in himself. To accept Christ is to be freed from the ordinances of the Law.

Therefore, through the cross Jesus not only *becomes* our peace; He also *makes* peace. In Himself He makes a new man from the two who were formerly separated. The world is no longer divided between Jew and Gentile. A new category has been added: the Church of Jesus Christ. "Therefore if any man be in Christ, he is a new creature: old things are passed away; behold, all things are become new" (II Cor. 5:17).

3. In Christ Jesus all are reconciled to God (vv. 16-17). Where there was formerly enmity, there must now be reconciliation. The enmity has been slain by Jesus' death on the cross. There is now a new body, the Church, a community of both Jews and Gentiles united under the headship of Christ. All that needed to be done has been done.

However, this reconciliation must be proclaimed and realized. For years the physical barrier in the Temple between Jews and Gentiles would continue to exist. For years the Law would continue to be a source of enmity, even threatening the unity of the Church. Therefore, the same Jesus who *became* our peace and who *made* our peace came also to *preach* peace, both to those who were far off and to those who were near. Jesus Christ preached peace through sending His Spirit upon His disciples and sending them into all the world to announce the message of reconciliation. And He continues to fill men with His Spirit so that this message will continue to be preached. His work of making peace has been accomplished for all eternity. But His work of preaching peace must go on until all have had the opportunity to hear.

4. In Christ Jesus we all have access to God (v. 18). Both Jews and Gentiles now have access, by the same Spirit, to God the Father. When Paul praised God for the spiritual blessings He gave us, he addressed his hymn of praise to the Father, Son, and Holy Spirit. And here, in summarizing Christ's work of reconciliation, he points out the ministry of each of the three persons of the Trinity. There need be no more foreigners with respect to God; all have the privilege of being introduced through Christ by one Spirit into the Holy of Holies. All former distinctions disappear in the body of Christ, "the fulness of him that filleth all in all."

III. NOW THEREFORE (2:19-22)

Verse 18 is a perfect transition into the last part of this passage. First, Paul points out what Gentiles were before Christ; second, he describes what God did for them through Christ; now he indicates what they have become. Because we have access by the same Spirit into God's presence, the old Temple, with its veil and Holy of Holies, becomes meaningless. In fact, we ourselves who form the new community of faith built on the foundation of the apostles and prophets grow into a new temple, a habitation of God through the Spirit. The Apostle's conclusions in these four verses are deep and moving. If we are willing to listen, we shall see our churches in a new and sobering perspective.

1. We are members of a new society (v. 19). Only someone who has been a foreigner, living in a strange country and never really able to break into the social structures that cut him off from others, can feel the import of Paul's words. We were strangers and we were foreigners. But this is over. We are no longer on the outside looking in. We are made fellow citizens with the saints, and members of God's household.

We have already seen how Paul has to pile up human terms in order to fully present spiritual truth. For instance, in this letter the Church is a body, a building, and a bride. No one of these images can give us an adequate idea of what the Church really is. And in verse 19, in trying to describe the new relationship which exists between Gentile and Jew, the Apostle uses two terms: "fellow-citizens" and "household." The first is a civic term; the second designates a family relationship.

We are fellow citizens. Citizenship always confers rights. The more powerful and rich a state, the greater will be the rights conferred upon its citizens. Paul himself is an example of this when he invokes Roman citizenship to avoid unjust treatment or to secure fair trial. As fellow citizens with the saints we have God's seal, the Holy Spirit, guaranteeing us all the rights and privileges of heaven itself. These rights are ours even while we are sojourners in a foreign state, still dominated by its unholy prince.

We are the household of God. Though we are thankful for our civic rights as citizens of a new society, we have the privilege of much more. The term "fellow citizen" is cold and official; the term "household" carries the warmth of a family relationship.

As citizens we have rights; as members of a family we find love, identity, and value. A state will seek to provide justice for its citizens; a family will offer concern, sympathy, and forgiveness.

The local church is meant to be a spiritual family. It is meant to provide for its members the spiritual counterpart of everything a family provides. A family provides nourishment; so should the church. It provides training and seeks to develop the potential of its children. It is willing to discipline, thus creating a sense of responsibility and a discernment of right and wrong. It enables its children to discover who they really are and gives them goals and purpose in life. And above all, it provides love. For without love, true life is not possible.

We can trust God to guarantee our rights as fellow citizens. But we ourselves must assume the responsibility of creating in our churches a genuine spiritual family so that our spiritual children will not be spiritually warped, unable to find their places in God's plan.

2. We have been built on the foundation of the apostles and prophets. (v. 20). First Paul tells what we are: fellow citizens in God's household. Now he talks about our foundation. Any construction is only as good as its foundation, as our Lord points out in His story about the wise man and the fool. Further, when a society of any kind loses its foundation, it is only a matter of time until it will begin to break down. "If the foundations be destroyed, what can the righteous do?" said the Psalmist (Ps. 11:3).

We must never forget that true harmony in the local church can be achieved only if each member is properly related to the foundation. You have seen what happens to buildings in which the foundation has not been properly laid; even the best of mortar, laid in the most skillful fashion, cannot hold the stones together. If your church has fissures in its walls, attention must first be given to the foundation; afterwards the problems can be patched up fairly easily.

The Church finds its foundation in both the apostles and the prophets. Though Jew and Gentile lose their identity to merge into a new community, neither is asked to forsake his spiritual heritage. The Church was born on the day of Pentecost, but its roots go into both the Old and the New Testaments; it is founded squarely on the whole Word of God. And the connecting link between the old and the new is Jesus Christ, who is here presented as the chief cornerstone, that part of the building which is cut out first and which becomes the test to determine whether the whole has been properly formed together.

3. We become a building (v. 21). When Gentiles and Jews become fellow citizens forming the household of God founded upon the apostles and prophets, they become a building. The image of the Church as a building is particularly appropriate, for it is especially fitted to the Church in its local and visible form, just as the idea of a body enables us to see certain aspects of the Church universal.

It is unfortunate that some who are engaged in the ministry we commonly call "church planting" seemingly fail to ask the basic question, "What, essentially, is a church?" Usually we define a church from the standpoint of form or organization. As a result, local churches are often basically no different from any other organization.

However, the image of a building teaches us that the church, before assuming a form, is essentially a *relationship*. The difference between a group of Christians who meet together regularly and a true local church is the same as the difference between a pile of stones and a building. A group of Christians become a church not when they decide to meet on Sunday morning, or write a constitution, or practice certain ordinances. They become a local church when each member commits himself spiritually to every other member, so that the whole becomes cemented together by the Holy Spirit into a spiritual entity, Jesus Christ being the chief cornerstone.

4. We grow into the temple of God (v. 21-22). Christians form a spiritual household; they are founded on the apostles and prophets; they thus become a spiritual building; this building grows into a temple of God.

To be sure, a building cannot grow the way a body grows. However, this building, which is the Church, can and must grow into something very special—the temple of God. When Jesus died, the veil in the Temple was ripped from top to bottom. Though the actual edifice in Jerusalem stood for another forty years, it was a temple in name only. The priests could sew together the torn veil, but they could not bring meaning to the Holy of Holies, for from the day of Pentecost to the present, the temple has been elsewhere.

All of us who know our Bibles know that the Christian is himself a temple of God, for the Holy Spirit dwells in him. Paul points this out in I Corinthians 6:19-20. But have we realized that the Church, even in its local expression, is also a temple of God? "Know ye not that ye are the temple of God, and that the Spirit of God dwelleth in you?" (I Cor. 3:16). Here Paul is not simply speaking of the Christian individually; he is speaking of the church at Corinth. And he goes on to say, "If any man defile the temple of God, him shall God destroy? for the temple of God is holy, which temple ye are." Any member of any local church who hinders his church from fulfilling its spiritual ministry finds himself in danger of being "destroyed," which means that God may prevent him from fulfilling his spiritual destiny.

Is your church a genuine spiritual building growing into a temple of the Lord? Are you built together with your fellow Christians to form a dwelling place of God through the Spirit? If there are cracks in the structure, do not try to solve the problem by putting on a little extra plaster. Real solutions will come from renewed commitment to our Lord, to the Scriptures, and to fellow Christians.

Questions for Discussion

1. What problems in our churches today would compare with the Jew-Gentile problem of the Early Church?

2. What was God's solution to the Jew-Gentile problem, and how can it bring solutions to problems that divide the Church today?

3. If the Church is a spiritual family, what steps can be taken to rediscover the idea of genuine community?

4. When does a group of Christians become a genuine local church?

5. How can the local church grow into a "habitation of God"?

5

The Mystery Unveiled

EPHESIANS 3:1-13

THE CHAPTER OUTLINED:

I. **Paul's Imprisonment**

II. **Paul's Calling**
1. God gave Paul the "dispensation" of preaching to the Gentiles
2. Paul's dispensation concerned divine revelation
3. Paul's knowledge of God's plan is evidence of this revelation
4. Paul's revelation is the mystery hidden in other ages but now made known

III. **Paul's Message**
1. The Gentiles were joint heirs
2. The Gentiles were a joint body
3. The Gentiles were joint partakers of God's promises

IV. **Paul's Ministry**
1. Paul was to preach to the Gentiles the unsearchable riches of Christ
2. Paul was to enlighted all about the mystery of the Church
3. Paul was to make known to the principalities and power the manifold wisdom of God

V. **Paul's Confidence**

Chapter 3 of Ephesians begins with the phrase, "For this cause," turning our thoughts back to the themes Paul developed in the first two chapters of the letter. There he explained that God's *plan* is to bring all things together under the authority of Christ. He said that God's *power* was demonstrated in raising Christ from the dead and establishing Him above all other authority. And he stated that God's *program* is to save by grace all who believe and to unite them—Jew and Gentile—in the same spiritual household. It is especially to this last idea that Paul makes reference here.

He does not finish his initial statement, however. After beginning, "For this cause I Paul, the prisoner of Jesus Christ for you Gentiles," his thoughts, full of the glory of the Church, do not permit him to continue. In fact, he does not return to his initial statement until verse 14. Yet, it would be a mistake to call the intervening verses a digression. In a sense, they are the heart of the letter, for they penetrate beyond the veil to reveal that the Church, though hidden in ages past, is central to God's plan. Everything Paul has revealed thus far focuses on it; everything he has to say in the following chapters grows out of it. In this intriguing passage the Apostle reveals that the Church is a part of God's eternal purpose and the instrument He has chosen to reveal His great wisdom to the principalities and powers in the heavenlies.

I. PAUL'S IMPRISONMENT (3:1)

These verses reveal the Church; they also reveal the Apostle. Here the pronouns change to the first person, and in this very personal passage Paul discloses, almost in wonder, that he was chosen to be God's instrument for revealing the unsearchable riches of Christ.

And yet, this man, who was chosen for what was perhaps the greatest mission accorded by God to men, is writing from a prison! In fact, he is in prison precisely because of the mission God gave him. He is a prisoner "for you Gentiles."

If Paul is in prison it is because he dared announce that Gentiles have the same spiritual rights as Jews. The Jews saw in this former Pharisee their greatest threat, and rightfully so. Wherever he went he met opposition. Finally they were able to seize him during his visit to Jerusalem, and would have murdered him on the spot had it not been for the intervention of the Roman soldiers guarding the Temple. At the time of this writing he has perhaps spent up to five years in captivity.

It is difficult to imagine how a man as active as Paul, chosen for such a lofty mission and in so much demand by the churches he founded, can remain in prison without complaint. However, Paul is not a prisoner of the Romans, and this he knows. He is a prisoner of Jesus Christ. Just as the Roman soldiers were only human instruments for accomplishing God's will in Christ's crucifixion, so these same Romans cannot retain Paul apart from his Lord's permission. He has already seen prison foundations shaken, doors opened, and bands loosened. He realizes that it is far better to be in prison in God's will than to be free and out of His will.

It is almost certain that Paul could not have written the letters of Ephesians and Colossians apart from his seclusion in prison. Perhaps their actual composition took only a short time so that Tychicus could deliver them when he returned to Asia Minor (Eph. 6:21). But their scope and vision reveal a perspective known only to those who have been pulled away from preoccupation with little things.

II. PAUL'S CALLING (3:2-5)

"Surely you have heard," writes the Apostle, "how God has assigned the gift of grace to me for your benefit." Thus Paul introduces to the Ephesian Christians this statement of his vocation.

1. God gave Paul the "dispensation" of preaching to the Gentiles (v. 2). The word "dispensation" is a rather old word meaning management, administration, or stewardship. We have already seen the word used in Ephesians 1:10, which says that God is the great Administrator of the universe and that He is managing things according to a plan which He purposed in Himself before the world began.

That chapter also taught that we have been given an inheritance in God's plan: an inheritance not in the sense of something future, but of being presently accorded a task in God's administration. God has delegated different responsibilities to His servants, making them in turn administrators in their areas of responsibility.

Paul's inheritance in God's plan included making known God's riches to the Gentiles and revealing the mystery of the Church.

2. Paul's dispensation concerned divine revelation (v. 3). Just as the Apostle did not choose his ministry, neither did he choose his message. He was not a philosopher or an inventor of a new religion, but a recipient of special revelation from God. Shortly after his conversion, rather than going to confer with the disciples in Jerusalem, he went into the desert of Arabia and there received the content of the good news he was to preach. Concerning this Gospel he stated, "I neither received it of man, neither was I taught it, but by the revelation of Jesus Christ" (Gal. 1:12).

3. Paul's knowledge of God's plan is an evidence of this revelation (vv. 3-4). He has already written "in few words" about the mystery of the Church. These few words are the passage in chapter 2 which reveals that Gentiles are to be included in the household of faith. "Whereby, when ye read, ye may understand my knowledge in the mystery of Christ," he states.

Paul implies that his message is a test of the spiritual discernment of his readers. "The natural man receiveth not the things of the Spirit of God: for they are foolishness unto him: neither can he know them, because they are spiritually discerned. But he that is spiritual judgeth all things" (I Cor. 2:14-15).

4. Paul's revelation is the mystery hidden in other ages but now made known (vv. 4-5). We have already seen that the term "mystery" does not refer to something mysterious or hard to understand, but to something formerly concealed but now revealed. In the Greek mystery religions the mystery was that which was beyond the veil dividing the initiated elite from others. In the Church there is no such division. We are all taken beyond the veil so that we can share fully all that God has chosen to reveal to us.

God's revelation, however, conforms to God's timing. The great mysteries of the New Testament are truths that could not be revealed until first of all, in "the fulness of time," God sent His Son to redeem us.

The Church is one of those mysteries "which in other ages was not made known unto the sons of men, as it is now revealed unto his holy apostles and prophets by the Spirit" (v. 5). The Church does not appear in the Old Testament; therefore, the prophets mentioned here are the prophets of the New. Though prophesied in the Gospels, the Church only came into existence on the day of Pentecost, when the Holy Spirit entered the believers and Peter preached his message of repentance.

Yet, though Peter was one of the apostles and prophets of the New Testament, even he did not fully understand at first what was going to happen. On a later occasion Paul had to reprimand him for not discerning the true nature of this new body, in which all men were to be accepted without discrimination. It took years for some of the Jewish Christians to accept Gentile brethren as fellow participants in the commonwealth of

God.

Though God no longer is giving men new revelations, His Spirit is nevertheless constantly revealing new truths of His children through the Word. Sometimes these are truths that have been obscure in our past experience. Then, in God's timing, we are ready for new insights. There is a lesson here that each Christian needs to learn: new insights into the Word are not the result simply of study, but also of willingness to obey. Some Jewish Christians were unable to comprehend the unsearchable riches of Christ simply because God's new revelation shattered their cherished traditions. Jesus pointed out once that we can have ears and still fail to hear.

III. PAUL'S MESSAGE (3:6)

Paul's calling was to be the administrator of the mystery of the Church; in verse 6 the content of this mystery, already revealed in chapter 2, is summarized in three points. The Gentiles are (1) equal heirs with God's chosen people, (2) equal members of Christ's body, and (3) equal partners in God's promise. This statement is even more striking in its original form, for there we find these three thoughts expressed in three terms each carrying the prefix "syn-," indicating perfect equality.

1. The Gentiles were joint heirs. Gentiles were formerly "aliens from the commonwealth of Israel," but now, in the Church, they are elevated to equal legal status. A man making a testament can choose to bestow a large sum on his favored children, reserving only a pittance for others. In God's new testament He makes no such distinction. Whatever is reserved for one will also be given to the others.

Writing to the Galatians, Paul said, "There is neither Jew nor Greek, there is neither bond nor free, there is neither male nor female: for ye are all one in Christ Jesus. And if ye be Christ's, then are ye Abraham's seed, and *heirs* according to the promise" (Gal. 3:28-29).

2. The Gentiles were a joint body. Though formerly "without Christ," they were, with the Jews, brought into a vital relationship with Christ. Our Lord has but one body, "the fulness of him that filleth all in all." The Church is the organism by which God is accomplishing His great eternal plan. Into this body are grafted all who are redeemed through faith; each without distinction becomes a member joined together by the same Spirit given to all. When we begin to understand the meaning of the term "joint body," we realize why Paul was so severe with Peter when Peter refused to break bread at the same table with Gentiles in the presence of the Jeru-

salem leaders (Gal. 2:11-16). Each local church *must* be a true manifestation of the universal Church, else it has no right to be called "Church."
There is orthodoxy of community as well as orthodoxy of doctrine.
Peter's action was a contradiction of the very essense of the message God
had committed to Paul and could therefore not be tolerated, even in the
person of the apostle who had been the human instrument for bringing the
Church into existence on the day of Pentecost.

3. The Gentiles were joint partakers of God's promise. Though formerly
"strangers from the covenants of promise," they could not claim God's
blessings on an equal basis with the Jews. Perhaps Paul here has reference
to the promise of the Holy Spirit, proclaimed on Pentecost by Peter, who
exclaimed, "The promise is unto you, and to your children, and to all that
are afar off, even as many as the Lord our God shall call" (Acts 2:39). This
promise was fulfilled when Peter announced the Gospel to Cornelius,
opening salvation to the Gentiles, and again when Paul taught the disciples
in Ephesus who had not yet heard of the Spirit's baptism.

However, we must not limit this statement, for Paul wants his readers
to realize that *all* the promises of God find their fulfillment in Christ and
are communicated by His Spirit to all believers, regardless of their racial or
religious background.

The distinctive element of the mystery committed to Paul was not that
Gentiles could share in God's blessings. This truth had already been revealed in the Old Testament and reiterated in the New. Paul quotes Hosea
in Romans 9:25, saying, "I will call them my people, which were not my
people; and her beloved, which was not beloved." This statement, like
many other passages of Scripture, shows that salvation is not limited to the
Jews.

The new element of the mystery of the Church is that Gentiles do not
have to become Jewish proselytes to receive salvation. Accepting Christ
does not mean being grafted into Judaism; rather, Jews and Gentiles become branches of Christ himself. Of the two, Jew and Gentile, God has
made *one new man.* In Christ's new society there are no second-class
citizens. We are all saved by faith in the same promises. We are all heirs of
a *new* testament. We are members of Christ's body.

IV. PAUL'S MINISTRY (3:7-12)

Every calling implies a ministry. Paul was called to administer the
mystery of the Church; the message he received was that the Gentiles are

fellow heirs, members of the same body, and fellow participants in God's promises. His ministry was to make known this message.

The word "minister" means servant. God's administrators are not to rule over the Church, as many have been guilty of doing in the past. They are to offer themselves in service to others, no matter how lofty their calling might be. In the words of Christ, they are not to be served, but to serve.

Paul here calls himself "less than the least of all saints." This is certainly not an expression of false humility; the Early Church probably possessed no equal of this great man of God, and Paul was not ignorant of his qualities. He doubtless alludes here to the greatness of God's grace offered to a man whose rebellion to the Spirit of God in persecuting the Christians could only be arrested by a miraculous intervention of Jesus Christ, striking him blind. How could he call himself other than "less than the least" if such dramatic measures were necessary to put him on the right path?

In fact, Paul implies that the power necessary to convert him, who formerly breathed out threatenings and slaughter against the disciples of the Lord, is of the same essence as that which raised Christ from the dead. For God's grace was given by the effectual working of His power—the same power "which he wrought in Christ, when he raised him from the dead" (Eph. 1:19-20).

Such great grace and power result in a great ministry, and the Apostle is fully aware of its scope. It is for the Gentiles, to be sure. Yet it is not limited to them, for it will reach to all men. But it will not even stop with men, for through this chosen man even the principalities and powers in the heavenlies will know, through the Church, the manifold wisdom of God.

1. Paul was to preach to the Gentiles the unsearchable riches of Christ (v. 8). Paul has been known throughout history as the Apostle to the Gentiles, for even though his message was given to all, it was he who almost single-handedly opened up the Gentile world to the Church. What a privilege it would have been to hear from his own lips the message that revolutionized the ancient world! In our own day, when so many of God's ministers are majoring in minors, what would happen to our churches if we would just start talking about the unsearchable riches of Christ?

The word "unsearchable" is formed from the noun for track, or trail. Christ's riches are unsearchable because man's mind could never have found them. The path by which these riches could reach man had to start from God; it had to be by revelation. And Paul had the privilege of indicating that path to the Gentiles.

2. Paul was to enlighten all about the mystery of the Church (v. 9). The scope of Paul's ministry widens to include all men. He is to make them see. To do this, he must bring to light the mystery that God committed to him; he must reveal to others the message revealed to him. The word translated "to make see" is where we get the term "photography." In order for an image to be inscribed on photographic film, light is necessary. The more light, the sharper the image, even on film which is not very sensitive. Paul's ministry, and ours, is not to try to make men more sensitive to the message. This is the work of the Holy Spirit. Our work is to bring enough light to record a clear image.

The word "fellowship" in verse 9 should be changed to "administration." The Apostle once again uses the term which designates his share in God's management of the universe, adding the idea that the God who called him is the same who created all things by Jesus Christ.

3. Paul was to make known to the principalities and power the manifold wisdom of God (vv. 10-11). The God who created all things created things visible and invisible. Several times already we have encountered the term "in the heavenlies," indicating the invisible world which exists beyond time and space as we know them. Paul's vision of his ministry is magnificent; he sees it as touching not only all men, but even the principalities and powers of the invisible world.

Many believe these principalities and powers refer to the unfallen angels who "desire to look into" the Gospel revealed from heaven (I Peter 1:12). It is, of course, true that the Church is a revelation of God's wisdom to all created beings. However, Paul's use of the terms "principalities" and "powers" in other parts of this letter would seemingly indicate that he here refers to the fallen hierarchy of spiritual beings that wrestle against the Christian and over which the risen Christ has been established (see Eph. 1:19-23 and 6:10-12).

If this is true, this verse provides an intriguing key to the reason God had to hide the great New Testament mysteries until after Christ was crucified and raised. Compare this passage with I Corinthians 2:7-8: "We speak the wisdom of God in a mystery, even the hidden wisdom, which God ordained before the world unto our glory: which none of the princes of this world knew: for had they known it, they would not have crucified the Lord of glory." It seems almost certain that the "princes of this world" are not human beings. Satan is the great prince of this world, and under him are the principalities and powers. Had they known God's wisdom, they would not have forced the crucifixion of Christ. We believe that Satan united all his forces to bring the Lord to His death, hoping to win the decisive battle in the age-long conflict between good and evil. But though Satan had the power of death, he was powerless before the Resurrection. Rather than thwarting God's great plan, he actually became an unknowing participant, and his unholy princes were no more than actors on the stage of the greatest of all dramas. Through the death and resurrection of Christ, God could justify all men, send His Spirit to dwell within them, and unite them all in Christ's body.

Imagine their great chagrin when Paul began to bring to light the mystery of the Church and in it the "manifold wisdom of God, according to the eternal purpose which he purposed in Christ Jesus our Lord." Through Christ, God has caused not only the wrath of man, but even that of angels, to praise Him.

V. PAUL'S CONFIDENCE (3:12-13)

Yes, the Ephesian Christians need not lose courage because of Paul's tribulations for them. After writing about God's eternal mysteries and their promised glory, how could he be upset because of present tribulations? He was the one who had learned not to faint, for "though our outward man perish, yet the inward man is renewed day by day. For our light affliction, which is but for a moment, worketh for us a far more exceeding and eternal weight of glory; while we look not at the things which are seen, but at the things which are not seen" (II Cor. 4:16-18).

True spirituality means seeing beyond the present; it means evaluating the immediate in terms of the eternal. Paul's trials were part of God's eternal plan, and this plan for Paul had included privileges no other men had known. If God's wisdom could bring to shame the principalities and powers united against His Son, certainly it could easily transform Paul's suffering into the glory of the Ephesian Christians.

Further, no prison cell could separate Paul from God. He had boldness, because in Christ he had free access to the throne of grace. This was the source of his confidence.

Can you not almost imagine the Apostle breaking out in laughter at the thought of the consternation brought into Satan's court when, one by one, the great mysteries of God were revealed? And can you not see him on his knees pouring himself out in praise for the grace that allowed him, less than the least of all saints, to bring to light the mystery of the Church and announce the unsearchable riches of Christ?

Questions for Discussion

1. Why is the Church called a mystery? Why were the mysteries of the New Testament hidden until Christ's death and resurrection?

2. What steps did God follow in the progressive revelation of His Church?

3. What was the new element about the Church in Paul's preaching?

4. Do you think many Christians understand today what the Church really is?

5. What can we do to make our local church and our denomination a true representation of the Church?

6. Why could Paul endure prison in confidence?

6
Filled with His Fullness

EPHESIANS 3:14-21

THE CHAPTER OUTLINED:

I.   The Father of the Whole Family

II. "That He Would Grant You"
   1. Strengthened by the Spirit
   2. Indwelt by Christ
   3. Filled with God's fullness

III. "Unto Him Be Glory"
   1. God is able
   2. "According to the power that worketh in us"
   3. "Unto him be glory"

The Apostle returns to the sentence broken off at the beginning of Ephesians 3 and uses it to lead into the second prayer of the letter. The phrase, "For this cause," refers to the previous chapters, especially to the revelation of God's plan incorporating Gentiles into the Church. God has done great things *for* the Gentiles; now Paul prays that God will do great things *in* them.

Paul's prison experience gave him the perspective necessary to see the entire scope of God's plan. But it did more; it allowed him to pray that God's plan might be realized in the lives of the Christians he knew. His ministry was not limited to preaching; it was also a ministry of praying. By proclaiming the mysteries of God, Paul could bring light, but only the Holy Spirit could bring power.

This is the second prayer included in the Ephesian letter, and both concern power. The emphasis, however, is different. In the first prayer (1:15-23) Paul asks that the eyes of their understanding may be opened, so that they may *know*. Here he prays that Christ may dwell in their hearts by faith, and he emphasizes *experience*. The first prayer lays stress on the knowledge of God's revelation; this one, on the realization of Christ's love.

We like to say that there is no power shortage for the Church. This statement is, of course, true; God's supplies are inexhaustible. As we look around us, though, we are forced to admit that many local churches are suffering from a serious shortage of spiritual power—not because the supply is short, but because the means of communication between God and the churches have deteriorated. Here is a prayer concerned with those lines of communication between God and His people.

I. THE FATHER OF THE WHOLE FAMILY (3:14-15)

"I bow my knees unto the Father." It is said that the customary position for Jews in prayer was to stand; only on occasions of great solemnity would they kneel. Whether Paul was speaking literally or figuratively is immaterial; the phrase shows us that the Apostle considered his prayer to be of special importance.

The prayer is addressed to the Father, "of whom the whole family in heaven and earth is named." In the original text the words "Father" and "family" come from the same root, indicating that God's spiritual family grows out of its relationship with Him. He is the "one God and Father of all, who is above all, and through all, and in you all" (4:6).

Some believe that Paul's statement about the Fatherhood of God refers to a universal Fatherhood growing out of the creation; they would include in God's family all men and angels, saved and lost. In the context, however, it seems more likely that Paul is referring to the great spiritual family that God has brought into existence through Christ. Paul has already talked of the middle wall of partition between Jew and Gentile being broken down, making of the two one new man, which he calls the household of God. This spiritual family includes all of God's true children, whether they are alive on the earth or have already been taken into the presence of our Lord Jesus Christ in the heavenlies.

Because God is the Father of this great family, He will provide its needs, especially its need of spiritual power. And the following prayer is certainly one of the most far-reaching ever uttered by one of God's children.

II. "THAT HE WOULD GRANT YOU" (3:16-19)

This is a prayer of superlatives. The words strain almost to the breaking point in their attempt to convey the Apostle's intent. The prayer begins with a staggering condition: Paul asks the Father to grant his requests "according to the riches of his glory." He asks that absolutely no limit be placed upon God's response to his request.

This letter says much about the glory of God. He is called the Father of glory. God's glory is linked with His infinity; it cannot be measured. The closer we get to God, the brighter is His glory, to the extent that mortal man has never seen the Father; creatures can only behold the glory emanating from His person. When Stephen looked up into heaven just before his martyrdom, he saw Jesus standing at the right of God. But Stephen could not see God; he could only see the glory.

If Paul had the boldness to ask "according to the riches of his glory," it is because he knew that the Heavenly Father wants to bless in exactly that way. God places no limit on His desire to grant us these requests. Limitation is from man's side, not God's.

After stating this initial condition, Paul presents three great requests, each linked to one of the members of the Trinity.

1. Strengthened by the Spirit (v. 16). Though we can never fully understand the Trinity, we learn in the Bible that each person of the Godhead is usually identified with a particular function. God the Father, the ultimate source of all things and the one to whom we address our prayers, is the one who ordains. God the Son, revealed as the Word, is the one who communicates and acts. Every time there is communication between God and man, it is through Christ. This is true also in the Old Testament, where Christ is revealed as the "Angel of the Lord."

God the Holy Spirit is the one who empowers. We see His power at work in the creation. We see it displayed in the miracles of the Old Testament. During His entire ministry, Jesus operated through the power of the Holy Spirit. After His death and resurrection He promised, "Ye shall receive power, after that the Holy Ghost is come upon you" (Acts 1:8).

What is power? Power is the ability to act according to one's will. Spiritual power is the ability God gives us through His Spirit to act according to His will. At times God shows His power through physical miracles, causing some people to assume that where there is spiritual power there must be miracles. This, however, is an unwarranted generalization. If God *wills* miracles, He gives His servants the power to perform them. But though miracles are rare in God's dealings with men, man's need for God's power is constant, for only through His power can we do His will.

Someone has said that Christianity is neither easy nor hard; it is impossible. From the human standpoint this is certainly true, for Christianity involves the supernatural work of bringing to life those who were dead in sins and transforming them into the image of Christ. It is a tragedy that so many Christians, while understanding theoretically what it means to be regenerated, try to live their lives much the same as someone who does not have Christ in him. When they face problems, their reaction is essentially the same as that of the man who knows nothing of the Holy Spirit's power. God's resources are available to all Christians, but they must be appropriated deliberately.

God's power works "in the inner man." This is the part of man which can live above the immediate and beyond personality. It is the place of man's spirit, where human nature comes into contact with the divine.

Doctors and psychologists tell us that the outer man can be healthy only when there is harmony in the inner man. Nearly all the illnesses produced by physical causes can be duplicated by an unhealthy spirit. The inner man determines what the outer will be. Health and happiness are the result of inner attitudes more than of circumstances.

Spirituality follows this same principle: the inner man determines what the outer will be. Christianity is not a matter of outwardly conforming to a system, but of being transformed from within. "Be ye transformed by the renewing of your mind," wrote Paul to the Romans, speaking of the Holy Spirit's working on the inner man (Rom. 12:2).

Before leaving this request for power we should notice one more point. Though the Spirit's power works individually, "in the inner man," Paul's prayer concerns the Church as a whole. God communicates His grace to us as individuals, but we are to live out our faith in communities. The preceding chapters revealed that the Church is a new household in which all the barriers between men have been removed. In chapter 4 we shall be exhorted to walk worthy of this great calling, so that the unity of the Church will become a visible reality. We must therefore not separate this prayer for the Spirit's strengthening from its context; God's power in us as individuals must show itself in our churches. When this power is present, it will make the spiritual unity of the Church a visible reality.

2. Indwelt by Christ (vv. 18-19). Paul's first request, therefore, is that we may be "strengthened with might by his Spirit in the inner man." His second is that Christ may dwell in our hearts by faith.

Though it is the Holy Spirit who empowers, the communication of this power is through Jesus Christ. In John 15 Jesus gave His disciples the image of a vine and its branches to help explain their relationship to Him. He is the vine; the disciples are the branches. Just as the branch must be in contact with the vine, so must the disciple abide in Him. When this is true, then the Holy Spirit's power fills the disciple's life in the same way as life-giving sap enters branches and produces fruit.

In the same context Jesus said of the Holy Spirit "He shall glorify me" (John 16:14). The lesson in these passages is obvious. We are not called to abide in the Holy Spirit, but in Christ. Our preoccupation should not be with the Holy Spirit, but with the Lord Himself. When the Church becomes overly preoccupied with the Holy Spirit, the result is usually division rather than unity. But when He is lifted up, He draws all men to himself and to one another.

How then does Christ dwell in us? To be sure, if we are genuinely regenerated, Christ is already in us, and for this reason many Christians have difficulty understanding the meaning of Paul's request. However, the Apostle seems to put the emphasis not on the *fact* of the indwelling Christ, but on the *way* we are to be indwelt in order to experience power. Christ is in all Christians. Our bodies are the temple of the Holy Spirit. Though He is in us, however, He does not necessarily rule in us. In order to have His power, the lines of spiritual communication must be open. A factory may possess generators of extraordinary capacity, but unless the switches are thrown there is no power.

The Apostle mentions two ways that Christ must dwell in us; these terms occur constantly in his writings: faith and love.

That Christ may dwell in your hearts by faith (v. 17). Faith is our response to God and His promises. It is our means of conscious contact with Him. Man's faith must be exercised through his will. We can choose to allow Christ to rule in us, or we can choose to work things out in our own way. Our faith is not a continuous and automatic response to God and His Word, but a series of choices growing out of particular situations. "Abide in me, and I in you," said Jesus. "As the branch cannot bear fruit of itself, except it abide in the vine; no more can ye, except ye abide in me" (John 15:4).

Being rooted and grounded in love (vv. 17-19). Faith is not the only line of communication. True, we must be joined to Christ by faith, but we must also be joined by love.

Love, like faith, is a quality that cannot exist independently. We are not asked to pray for love any more than we are asked to pray for faith; we are commanded to love. The kind of love mentioned here is more than a nice feeling; spiritual love grows out of a will to love.

Paul prays that we may be rooted and grounded in love. We can be *rooted* in love because spiritual love is a growing experience. Our love cannot remain static; to stop growing is to risk destruction. We can be *grounded* in love because spiritual love is solid. Though situations change, love never fails. It is not subject to variable emotions and impulses.

All Christians know they are to love. Yet is it not obvious that much of our talk about love is an indication of its absence? How can we be rooted and grounded in love? Paul's prayer reveals that our love must grow out of Christ's love. We can love only because He loved. The starting point for experiencing love is not others, but Christ. In knowing His love, we can love others.

Paul makes two requests concerning love, both of which are startling. First, he prays that we may be able to comprehend Christ's love. To comprehend means to grasp, or take in. But how can finite man grasp the love of an infinite Christ? Its dimensions are staggering. It is infinitely wide, long, deep, and high.

Naturally we shall never, throughout eternity, be able to grasp the infinity of Christ's love. Yet, Paul never prayed for impossible things. He fully expected God to answer this prayer. He is therefore not asking that man in his finiteness be able to comprehend infinity, but that God's infinity might fill man's finiteness. We can never know the breadth, length, depth, and height of Christ's love with respect to *His* experience, but we can know it with respect to *ours*.

Further, we can comprehend this "with all the saints." Paul not only asks that the breadth, length, depth, and height of our personal experience be filled with Christ's love, but he also prays this for the whole Church.

Man can never enter into God's infinity, but God can enter into man's finiteness. Christ gives His love without reserve; only man's limitations prevent full experience of that love. But though limited at any point of time, man's capacity is limitless. And the more he discovers, the greater is his capacity for further discovery.

Paul's second request about love is that we might know that which surpasses knowledge. To grasp that which is beyond our ability to grasp, to know that which is beyond our ability to know—this is what Paul covets for believers. Of course, this knowledge cannot be simply intellectual. We do not have to understand love in order to know it. We can know by experience. Many of the things we know we do not fully understand. In fact, full understanding usually can only come through experience.

What extraordinary requests! Love, as faith, must be exercised, but it cannot be self-generated; it must come from Christ. We love when we are able to grasp Christ's love in its overwhelming dimensions. We can know by actual experience that which will always be beyond our capacity to understand. And to this extent we are "filled with all the fulness of God."

3. Filled with God's fullness (v. 19). In his prison cell Paul was filled with thoughts of God's fullness. In raising Christ, God the Father put Him above all principalities and powers and made Him the head of the Church, "the fulness of him that filleth all in all" (1:23). When Jesus Christ is exalted in our lives above all other authority that seeks to dominate or enslave, then we know in actual experience this fullness of God.

When the term "fullness" is used about God, it carries the ideas of control and completeness. God does not fill men in the way that we fill buckets. God can only fill to the extent that He controls. Man is a free being; God never violates man's freedom. As we progressively submit areas of our lives to Him, He fills them. His great plan is that all things, through Christ, will be brought under His authority.

The idea of fullness is developed in a remarkable way in Paul's letter to the Colossians, written at the same time as Ephesians. Three verses from the first two chapters of that letter show God's way of transforming Christians without destroying their own personalities: "It pleased the Father that in him [Christ] should all fulness dwell" (Col. 1:19). "Christ in you, the hope of glory" (Col. 1:27). "And ye are complete in him"

(Col. 2:10).

All fullness in Christ; Christ in me; completeness in Him. God's fullness is an experience that cannot be explained; it can only be experienced. And those who have experienced God's complete filling know the deep satisfaction that it brings. Many human experiences bring a sense of temporary fulfillment. But human satisfaction never lasts. "Jesus said unto them, I am the bread of life: he that cometh to me shall never hunger; and he that believeth on me shall never thirst" (John 6:35).

III. "UNTO HIM BE GLORY" (3:20-21)

After such a prayer the Apostle can no longer restrain himself; in a spectacular display of spiritual exaltation he bursts into a doxology of praise that vibrates with God's infinity and breaks out into eternity. His use of language leaves us breathless; to praise God he constructs what someone has called a "super-superlative." It takes three words in our English version to translate one of his: "exceedingly abundantly above."

The letter to the Ephesians begins with a hymn of praise; its first half ends with this little doxology which is just as sweeping in its scope as the beginning hymn. In his letter to the Ephesians Paul will now turn to the practical outworkings of the truths he has just revealed. He will emphasize how we, who are members of Christ's body, ought to *walk*. However, let us not become preoccupied with our walk to the extent that we lose sight of God's glory. In our effort to work out these truths in real-life situations, may we remember that His power is within us. And when we face seemingly impossible situations, may we turn to Him who is able to do exceedingly abundantly more than we can ask or think.

1. God is able (v. 20). God's power is not limited in any way by His person. Over and over again we read in the Scriptures that with Him all things are possible. He is the Omnipotent. He can never over-expend Himself. Whatever He does, there is always an infinite reserve. He is able.

Further, God's power is not limited by our finiteness. He can do more than we can ask or think. Though He will not violate our will, He is not limited by our weakness. We are not obligated to try to decide what God can do in a given situation, or to figure out how He ought to do it. We can trust. And the very act of trusting unlooses His infiniteness. "Likewise the Spirit also helpeth our infirmities: for we know not what we should pray for as we ought: but the Spirit itself maketh intercession for us with groanings which cannot be uttered" (Rom. 8:26).

2. "According to the power that worketh in us" (v. 20). God is able because God possesses power. There are many things we think we would like to do, but we do not possess the power to do them. God knows no limitations; what He wills He can do. Further, His power is already at work. It is not on reserve some place, waiting to be tapped. It is in the person of His Spirit, who is already acting. Finally, this power is in us. When we need God's help, we can have it immediately. He has come to live within us and His power is available in us. If we lack the power to be and do what He has willed, it is simply because we are not appropriating what we already possess.

3. "Unto him be glory" (v. 21). Our God is the Father of glory. He showed His glory to men through Jesus Christ. "We beheld his glory, the glory as of the only begotten of the Father" (John 1:14).

But men can no longer see God's glory in Jesus Christ. Jesus has returned to the Father and has sent His Spirit upon men in order that His body, the Church, be formed. If men can no longer see God's glory in Jesus Christ, they are to see it in the Church.

Thus far in this letter we have learned much about the Church. We shall learn more. Should we not pause between the doctrinal and practical portions of this letter to exclaim, with Paul, "Unto him be glory in the church!" The Church is the place where men must be able to see God's glory. And the Church, Christ's body, is visible only in local churches. Yours is one of those churches which stands before a watching world. And you are a member of that church.

When people see your church, do they see God's glory?

Questions for Discussion

1. What is spiritual power? Why must the Christian live by the power of the Holy Spirit?

2. If God is more interested in the inner man than in the outer, why are most of our prayers, unlike Paul's, concerned with physical things?

3. Is faith a gift of God or our response to God's gifts? Explain.

4. What does it mean to know that which goes beyond knowledge? Why is Paul so concerned that Christians know love?

5. In what way does God fill the Christian?

7

Unity and Diversity

EPHESIANS 4:1-10

THE CHAPTER OUTLINED:

I. Keeping the Unity
1. Their walk is to be worthy of their calling
2. Believers are to walk in humility and patience
3. Believers should try to keep the unity

II. One Body
1. One body, one Spirit, one hope
2. "One Lord, one faith, one baptism"
3. One Father, above all, through all, in all

III. Unto Every One
1. Gifts and grace
2. Gifts and the ascended Christ

One of the key phrases of the letter to the Ephesians is "in the heavenlies." Formerly dead in sins, the believer has been given life in Christ and raised up to sit in heavenly places. But though spiritually he has been translated into another world, his feet remain firmly planted in this one. And having formerly walked "according to the course of this world," he must now walk in a new way. Being born is one experience; learning to walk is another.

The chapters we shall now study concern the Christian's walk. As in many of his other letters Paul divides Ephesians into two major parts, one doctrinal and the other practical. Chapters 1 to 3 concern the Church in its revelation; chapters 4 to 6, the Church in its relationships. Neither is complete without the other. We must do more than master the revelation of the mystery of the Church; we are expected to walk in a manner worthy of our high calling. We cannot pretend to have learned the doctrine unless our walk conforms to our belief.

The Christian must learn to walk, but he is not to walk alone. He walks as a member of a great spiritual family, and his walk should be a testimony of two basic characteristics of the Church, which Paul brings out here at the beginning of the practical portion of the letter. These characteristics are unity and diversity. The Church is one. But it is composed of widely differing people who have received differing gifts; the unity of the Church is to manifest itself through this diversity.

No local church can be a true expression of the universal Church if it fails to exhibit both unity and diversity. Unity is not uniformity; a healthy church will be able to incorporate differences among its members. God is a God of infinite diversity, and no two of His creatures are exactly alike. Further, diversity is not division; in spite of our differences, "by one Spirit are we all baptized into one body, whether we be Jews or Gentiles, whether we be bond or free; and have been made all to drink into one Spirit" (I Cor. 12:13).

I. KEEPING THE UNITY (4:1-3)

Once again Paul reminds his readers that he is the prisoner of the Lord. When he was with them he could be their example of the way a believer ought to walk; now he can only beseech them by letter. A little later in this chapter he will list specific commands. Here he lays down some basic principles concerning the walk of God's people.

1. Their walk is to be worthy of their calling (v. 1). "Walk worthy of the vocation wherewith ye are called." The word "vocation" has come to mean an occupation, but formerly it simply meant a calling. Paul is not referring to a special group of Christians who are engaged in a specific kind of ministry; he is referring to all who have been called from spiritual death to new life, and from being aliens to citizenship in God's household.

"Ye are no more strangers and foreigners, . . . therefore . . . walk worthy." There must be correspondence between the call and the walk. Having received new life in Christ, believers are no longer to walk in the lust of the flesh. Having been brought into a new fellowship, they must be worthy representatives of their new spiritual community.

We read in another passage that "we are unto God a sweet savour of Christ, in them that are saved, and in them that perish" (II Cor. 2:15). This verse seems to indicate that something about a believer should make him distinctive, and that it is something different from mere appearance. This distinctiveness is connected with his walk. "Now thanks be unto God, which always causeth us to triumph in Christ, and maketh manifest the savour of his knowledge by us in every place" (II Cor. 2:14).

2. Believers are to walk in humility and patience (v. 2). Though their calling is high, their walk is to be lowly; in this they are to be worthy of their Lord's example. In a similar passage the Apostle states, "Let nothing be done through strife or vainglory; but in lowliness of mind let each esteem other better than themselves." Then as an example of this kind of attitude he presents Jesus Christ, who "made himself of no reputation, and took upon him the form of a servant" (Phil. 2:3, 7).

Four terms are used in Ephesians 4:2 to indicate the way the believer should walk: "lowliness," "meekness," "longsuffering," and "forebearance." Lowliness is the inner quality of humility; meekness is humility in its expression towards others. Longsuffering is the inner quality of patience; forebearance is patience in its expression towards others.

We should notice several things about these qualities. First, they are not merely natural personality traits. All Christians, through the Holy Spirit, can behave with humility, but no one is really naturally humble. All Christians can have patience, but no one is patient naturally. We must not excuse our lack of humility and patience by saying, "I'm just not that way," because as a matter of fact no one is down inside.

Second, these qualities do not imply weakness; they indicate true spiritual strength. No one who has really found himself with respect to His God has to create an illusion of self-glory or vaunt himself before others. No one who is willing to believe that God has a plan for his life which even includes irritations has to lose his temper when things go wrong or others fail to fit into his pattern.

Third, unless we are willing for our relationships with fellow Christians to be humble and patient, our churches cannot express unity through diversity. These qualities are indispensable. The Church is not a conglomeration of people seeking to retain their independence, but rather a spiritual fusion of new men and women molded together by God's Spirit. The spirit of independence was the cause of the first sin; we are free, but never autonomous.

3. Believers should try to keep the unity (v. 3). Unity is already a spiritual reality in the Church of Jesus Christ. In the entire first part of his letter Paul carefully showed how Jesus Christ, our peace, has made one new man, having broken down the middle wall of partition and abolished enmity.

The command here in verse 3 states that believers must keep, or guard, the unity—this unity that Jesus has already accomplished. Scriptures give absolutely no justification for the tendency of Christians to condone division in their churches by saying that true unity is invisible. Of course it is—in the invisible Church! But our churches are very visible, and unity in the visible church must also be visible. Christ has made peace, but we must keep it by being humble and patient in our daily walk.

Unity in the Church was the subject of the prayer Jesus prayed just before His death. He did not simply pray for his immediate disciples. He prayed "for them also which shall believe on me through their word; that they all may be one; as thou, Father, art in me, and I in thee, that they also may be one in us: that the world may believe that thou hast sent me" (John 17:20-21). We must not think that the unity for which Jesus prayed is only invisible and spiritual. It is something the world should be able to see. The world cannot see the invisible unity of the Church; it can only witness the visible unity of Christians, or the lack of it. Only by keeping the unity of the Church can we really expect the world to believe that Jesus has been sent by the Father.

How is unity to be kept? It must be bound fast, or it will easily slip away. The bond that will guard it safely is called peace. Jesus has made peace, making unity possible. We, too, are to be peacemakers, making unity a reality. A peacemaker and a peace-seeker are not the same. Some Christians flee from one difficult situation to another, always seeking peace. Others, bearing one another's burdens, have that amazing capacity of bringing peace.

Most division among Christians, though often justified doctrinally, is caused by basic attitudes reflecting the sinful nature. Among the works of the flesh are quarrels, jealousy, bad temper, rivalry, factions, party spirit, and envy (Gal. 5:19-21, Phillips). Love and peace, essential to unity, come from the Holy Spirit and are evidence of His fullness.

II. ONE BODY (4:4-6)

The Church's unity is based on its uniqueness. Because there is but one Church, unity in the local church and among local churches is possible, for each local church is simply a visible manifestation of the invisible reality. The local church has meaning because it is an expression of the universal. To the degree that local congregations and denominations become spiritually independent, they cease to express the glory of the true Church.

Unity is not to be confused with union. Many "churches," having departed from truth, try to compensate for their lack of genuine spiritual unity by organizational union. However, just as it is impossible for all Christians to be members of the same local church, so it is undesirable for all local churches to merge into one huge worldwide denomination. Unity must not violate diversity. We have families of people, and we should have families of churches. The world is not scandalized by diversity, but rather by spiritual division. True churches, while existing in different denominations, can nevertheless present a true image of the whole.

Though churches and denominations are many, the true Church is one, and Ephesians 4:4-6 presents the base of unity. This base is composed of seven unique realities, including and grouped around the three persons of the Trinity. Some believe this statement to have been a kind of creed of the early Christians.

1. One body, one Spirit, one hope (v. 4). There is one body. It is difficult to imagine a more fitting image of the Church. Just as the body is one, so is the Church. Just as the body has many members, so does the Church. In spite of its diversity, every part is joined to the head, and each member is dependent upon every other member in order to function properly. No member can say that it has no need of the others. Nor must any member lose its sense of identity or feel useless because it is not like the others.

There is one Spirit. The Holy Spirit is the one who convicts men of their need of Christ. He brings life to the believer through new birth and unites believers in the same body. He is the one who fills the body with

Christ's life, just as branches receive life from a vine through the sap that penetrates every part of them.

There is one hope. Hope looks to the future. In this matter we have seen that the Holy Spirit is the down payment of our future inheritance. Because we have been baptized into one Spirit to form one body, we have confidence that what God has begun in us will be brought to perfection, so that we shall one day be a part of "a glorious church, not having spot, or wrinkle, or any such thing" (5:27). We should not think of our inheritance so much in what we shall get, but in what we shall become. We are all destined to perfection, for God is now at work in all believers, which means that we all participate in the same great hope.

2. "One Lord, one faith, one baptism" (v. 5). There is one Lord, He is the great Rock upon which the Church is built. "For other foundation can no man lay than that is laid, which is Jesus Christ" (I Cor. 3:11). He is also the head of the Church. Every church founded upon Christ and under His headship is an expression of His uniqueness. There are many false Christs, but only one true, before whom one day every knee shall bow and every tongue confess Him Lord (Phil. 2:10-11).

There is one faith. Just as hope looks to the future, faith looks to the past. Just as hope is connected to the Holy Spirit and our future inheritance, faith is connected to our Lord and His death and resurrection. There are many "faiths," but only one true "faith," for God had but one Son, who came into our world to die once for all men and all times. To separate faith from its historical roots is to make it vain subjectivism.

There is one baptism. Christians profess their faith in Christ through baptism, which is the act of identifying personally with His death and resurrection. Since there is only one Lord and only one faith, there can be only one baptism: that which identifies us with our Lord. Any other kind of baptism is meaningless.

3. One Father, above all, through all, in all (v. 6). Though God is in three persons, He is one. Though He is one, He is trinity. We never see any person of the Godhead acting independently. Paul began his series of seven by stating the uniqueness of the Holy Spirit. Then he said there is one Lord. Now He comes to the ultimate source of all things, God the Father. But in revealing the uniqueness of the Father, his thoughts again break into a trinity of expression, for the Father is above all, through all by Jesus Christ the Word, and in all by the Holy Spirit.

God is the source of all things, but He is the source of the Church in particular. He is the one who fills all things; He is the Father, in whom the spiritual fatherhood has its existence. Because God is the Father of all, only a spiritually united Church can exhibit His uniqueness.

The Apostle presents the Trinity in a different order from most scriptural statements. Instead of Father, Son, and Holy Spirit, the names are reversed. This is because all members of the true Church meet God in this order. First, the Holy Spirit performs His work in their hearts, convicting them of their need. Then they meet Christ, who stands at the door of their hearts, and invite Him to come in. Through Him they have free access to the Heavenly Father.

Those who have met God personally usually have no real problems with the doctrine of the Trinity.

III. "UNTO EVERY ONE" (4:7-10)

There is one body, but it is composed of many members. "For the body is not one member, but many" (I Cor. 12:14). After emphasizing the Church's unity, based on its unique sevenfold foundation, Paul turns to its diversity with the phrase, "But unto every one of us." Spiritually we are one, but we are also many, and God deals with us not as impersonal units but as distinct individuals.

This passage indicates that God's grace is not communicated through the Church to its members, as in the traditional Roman Catholic conception with its sacraments. It is communicated to the Church individually through its members. God fills individuals with His fullness, and these individuals in turn compose the Church. The Church is not primarily an institution, but a body in which each member has access to the throne of grace. To be sure, this grace is to strengthen the body, and not just the individual Christian. But it comes directly from God to the individual.

The Apostle introduces the idea of diversity by speaking of spiritual gifts. Humanly speaking, diversity appears in many ways; for instance, each member has his own personality, tastes, and convictions. But spiritually, diversity results in God's granting different gifts to His children.

1. Gifts and grace (v. 7). Paul seems to make a distinction between the gifts of Christ to the Church and the gifts of the Holy Spirit to individuals. The ascended Christ gives gifts to the Church in the form of people, called apostles, prophets, evangelists, pastors, and teachers. The Holy Spirit gives gifts to individuals in the form of "grace" to empower and equip them for the kind of ministry they are to perform in the Church. In fact, the gifts of the Spirit are designated by the term "charisma," which comes from the word for grace, and they refer to supernatural endowments rather than to entities in themselves. On the other hand, the word used for the gifts of Christ is the normal word for gift and refers to something that exists in itself.

There is a great deal of discussion seeking to distinguish between natural gifts or talents, on the one hand, and spiritual gifts on the other. Many Christians are puzzled as to whether their abilities, such as facility of speech or musical talents, are natural or spiritual. We often hear that every Christian has been given at least one spiritual gift, and many Christians spend years trying to determine what it is. Much of this discussion is meaningless and confusing. All of us have natural abilities and talent, which God expects us to offer to Him. To the extent that we are filled with the Spirit, our natural gifts become spiritual. The Holy Spirit does not give talents; He gives grace which endows our talents with supernatural power. To be sure, some of the Holy Spirit's gifts have been spectacular, such as the ability to perform miracles. But even there the gift was not the miracles, but the grace which allowed ordinary men to perform extraordinary tasks.

God's grace is given "to all of us." This means that every Christian receives the divine favor necessary to equip him for his spiritual ministry, if he is willing to trust God for it. In this sense, all Christians can be "charismatic." It is extremely unfortunate that the term "charismatic" has come to be limited to a certain category of Christians who engage in a practice which not everyone would attribute to the Holy Spirit. God's grace is not limited. It is for all.

But though no Christians are excluded from God's grace, they receive grace in proportion to Christ's gifts. "But unto every one of us is given grace according to the measure of the gift of Christ." Remember, the gift of Christ is the Christian himself, given to the Church to perform a specific ministry. In our next chapter we shall discuss this in more detail. All gifts require grace; some gifts require exceptional grace. But no matter what ministry we are called upon to perform, God's spiritual resources are equal to the need.

2. Gifts and the ascended Christ (vv. 8-10). The "gifts unto men" are associated with the ascended Christ. This passage quotes Psalm 68:18, which presents a victorious king in his triumphal procession, leading captives and distributing gifts. Significantly, this Psalm was read at Pentecost in the synagogues.

Many interpretations for these verses have been suggested, but the traditional view of the Early Church fathers, which identified the "lower parts of the earth" with hades, seems best.

Christ descended into the "lower parts of the earth." Before Jesus' death the spirits of the dead were kept in hades, a place of suffering for the lost and of comfort for the saved. The most graphic presentation of hades is Jesus' story of the rich man and Lazarus. After His death and before His resurrection Jesus descended into hades to announce to the saved that their redemption was accomplished and that they could now enter into the very presence of God.

Christ ascended, leading captives with Him. The captives I believe to be the spirits of those saved before the death of Christ. In ascending in triumph into heaven, Christ led them into the presence of God.

Christ gave gifts to men. The ascended Christ, "having spoiled principalities and powers" (Col. 2:15), could now establish His own authority in the Church by sending representatives to govern His new spiritual society. Just as victorious kings establish governors over their territories, so Christ gives men to the Church to be spiritual authorities. To be sure, each member of His body is spiritually united with Him and benefits individually from His fullness. But through those whom He has given to the Church, His authority is extended, so that in ever-widening circles He might "fill all things."

The Church's unity is based on the uniqueness of Christ. He is the head of the Church. Since His ascension, however, Christ sits at the right hand of God; He is no longer personally with His disciples. But though Jesus Christ cannot be personally with His followers scattered throughout the entire earth, He has sent His representatives wherever the Church has been established. The Church is one, but it manifests itself in a great diversity of ministries. And amazingly enough, as we shall see in the next chapter, it is through this diversity of ministry that unity becomes a reality.

Questions for Discussion

1. What do we mean when we say that unity is not uniformity? Can people have real spiritual unity if they do not agree on details?

2. In "keeping the unity," how can we distinguish between that which is essential and that which is secondary?

3. Do you think it is possible for churches to express true spiritual unity without belonging to the same denominations?

4. Why must we have a clear vision of the Church's uniqueness in order to preserve its unity?

5. What is the difference between "grace" and "gifts" in this passage?

8

The Church's Ministers

EPHESIANS 4:11-16

THE CHAPTER OUTLINED:

  I. "And He Gave"

  II. Why He Gave
     1. The immediate purpose of the ministry
     2. The goal of the ministry
     3. The results of the ministry

  III. A Growing Church
     1. Christ is the source of Church growth
     2. To grow, the Church must be "fitly joined
          together and compacted"
     3. Growth can only be "in love"

Paul makes a distinction between grace and gifts. The Holy Spirit gives grace to Christians, and the Lord gives Christians to the Church in the form of apostles, prophets, evangelists, pastors, and teachers. In this chapter we shall examine the nature of the Church's ministries and their purpose in the body of Christ.

In any discussion involving spiritual gifts and ministries, it is helpful to read I Corinthians 12:4-6, where Paul distinguishes between gifts, administrations, and operations.

First, there are different gifts, but the same Spirit. Since the Holy Spirit is the one who supplies power for the Church, His gifts are in the form of grace to the individual Christian. The gifts of the Spirit are not things in themselves, but ability to use what we already possess—our minds, our tongues, our talents—in a supernatural way, according to His will. Many of these spiritual gifts have been miraculous; all spiritual gifts are supernatural, even though they express themselves through our natural abilities.

Second, there are different administrations, but the same Lord. The word "administration" is normally translated "ministry." The Lord, as head of the Church, gives men to the Church in the person of apostles, prophets, evangelists, pastors, and teachers to build up the body.

Third, there are different operations, but the same God. The word "operation" could be translated "activity" and probably refers to the exercising of the ministries mentioned above. Since God the Father is the source of authority in the Church, those performing a ministry must do so in His authority. In the Early Church the positions of authority were grouped under two main titles, "elder" and "deacon." Even when a person receives spiritual gifts and is given to the Church in a ministry, he can only minister to the extent that the local church recognizes his authority. To exercise gifts without the accompanying authority is to invite confusion and division.

It is not our purpose here to determine what gifts are still given to the Church today. No matter what names we use to designate our leadership, it is evident that as long as the Church exists, the Holy Spirit will continue to give supernatural grace to Christians, the Lord will continue to supply the Church with its necessary ministries, and God will continue to accord authority to those whom the churches recognize as their spiritual leaders.

I. "AND HE GAVE" (4:11)

Paul presents a list of five ministries which the Lord accorded the

Church when He ascended into heaven to assume its headship. We should read verse 11 as follows: "He gave some *to be* apostles, prophets, evangelists, pastors and teachers." He did not present these gifts to the men, but rather He gave these men to the Church.

Many commentators divide the list into two pairs, apostle and prophet being one, evangelist and pastor-teacher being the other. The first pair concerns the founding of the Church. We read in 2:20 that the Church is built on the foundation of apostles and prophets. The second pair concerns the continuation of the Church. In the second pair the construction of the original text indicates that the ministries of pastoring and teaching are embodied in the same person.

In a narrow sense, the apostles and prophets were exclusively for the New Testament church. The original apostles received their commission directly from the Lord. The prophets received their message from heaven. In practice, however, the Church throughout history has needed all five of these gifts.

The Church needs apostles. The term means "sent ones"; today we call them missionaries, and the Lord gives them to plant the Church where it does not exist or where it once existed but since disappeared.

The Church needs prophets. The prophet is the one who proclaims divine revelation. The Church does not need new revelations; God has given us His eternal Word, and woe to those who add to it! But the Church will always need those who can boldly proclaim God's revelation to men. In a world which has lost its sense of absolutes, the Church needs men who, without cutting themselves off from the world in which they live, can still affirm without compromise, "Thus saith the Lord."

The Church needs evangelists. Whereas the prophet proclaims revelation, the evangelist announces the good news. He is the one the Lord gives to the Church with the gift of moving people to a decision to accept Him into their lives. Evangelists are often criticized for appealing to men's emotions; how else, however, do most people decide anything? To be sure, a true decision for Christ must be an intelligent one.

The Church needs pastors. The pastor is the shepherd. He is the one who leads the flock and, like the great Pastor, cares for them individually.

The Church needs teachers. The teacher is the one who knows the whole Word of God so that he can give Christians a balanced diet of truth, allowing normal growth. He must also guard against errors, usually the result of separating certain truths from their scriptural context and deforming them. The true teacher will avoid sensationalism and will seek balance.

In order for a local church to be a faithful expression of the universal Church, it must have leadership and must recognize that this leadership is a gift of the Lord. Concerning these gifts to the Church, Paul states, *"God hath set some in the church"* (I Cor. 12:28). To refuse to respect the spiritual authority of those who are in leadership is to refuse God, and the result is confusion.

For many years there has been a reaction against all kinds of authority, frequently even in the Church. This refusal of spiritual authority is especially evident in congregationally governed churches. We should understand, however, that even in a church that is congregationally governed, final authority is never in the hands of the congregation. Authority is always in God, who Himself gives the local church its leaders, no matter what its system of government may be.

In a congregationally governed church, leaders are appointed by the local church, rather than being imposed by a bishop or a committee outside the local group. But though the local congregation appoints its leaders, it must realize that their authority comes from God. In the local church all members are equal before God in spiritual worth, but not in authority.

II. WHY HE GAVE (4:12-15)

Our risen Lord has given His Church apostles, prophets, evangelists, pastors, and teachers. Why? It is so that through them He can accomplish certain things. Everything God does is for a purpose, and the purpose of the ministry is stated in the verses that follow.

1. The immediate purpose of the ministry (v. 12). This verse contains three phrases: "the perfecting of the saints," "the work of the ministry," and "the edifying of the body of Christ." We should not understand these as three purposes distinct in themselves. Rather, each phrase grows out of the preceding one. Saints are to be perfected in order to do the work of the ministry, and the work of the ministry is to result in the edifying of the body.

For "perfecting of the saints." Some have misunderstood the meaning of this phrase by taking "perfecting" to mean "sanctifying." To be sure, Christians are to be made holy, but the word used here means "to equip." Ministers are to perfect the saints in the sense of equipping or outfitting them for the service they are to render.

In other words, the immediate objective of the ministry is to train others. It is not simply to fill Christians' heads with knowledge, even though knowledge is a necessary part of this training. The Lord's ministers are placed in the body for the purpose of helping others fulfill *their* purpose. Every minister is to multiply himself in the lives of those who are placed in his care.

We tend to create all kinds of standards for our spiritual leaders. The ideal minister, according to many, is personable, well-educated, a good organizer, and a compelling preacher. Sometimes we are more impressed by a minister's style than by what he is actually accomplishing. According to verse 12, however, the important thing is not whether a minister is timid or outgoing, polished or clumsy, scholarly or self-taught. It is whether he is doing the right thing. He is given to the Church to train the saints. Unless he is doing this, he may be quite efficient, but he is hardly effective.

For "the work of the ministry." Why should the saints be equipped? The answer is so that they, too, may do the work of the ministry.

This statement implies two things. First, it implies that the training given to saints should be given in view of the ministry they are to perform. The weakness of some Christian education is that it is an end in itself. The training of the disciples was ideal in that Jesus trained them "on the job." They could test their training immediately in real-life situations. One of the successes of the communist movement is its insistence on giving people just enough training to do the job. When they fall flat on their faces, they are ready to run back to their leaders for more training. One of their sayings is, "It is better to do something imperfectly than to do nothing perfectly." Today we have far too many churches full of spiritual perfectionists whose Christian service consists of sitting on a pew for an hour every Sunday morning, then criticizing others for the mistakes they make.

Paul's statement in verse 12 also implies that service must be provided for those who are trained. It is no use helping someone develop his gifts if we do not let him use them. Further, most people will not be satisfied with the kind of service which consists only of passing out hymnals or counting offerings. They, too, must be involved in helping others. Every ministry, all down the line, is to equip others; the principle of multiplication is to be preserved at every level. Naturally, in every ministry we sometimes have to do things that are relatively uninteresting. But every true ministry has as its primary purpose serving others.

For "**edifying the body of Christ**." No ministry is to be an end in itself. We serve so that the body of Christ can be strengthened. Some Christians are looking for a ministry only because they want a sense of personal fulfillment. True ministries seek the fulfillment of the whole body of Christ.

The word "edify" means to build up. Just as Paul mixed his metaphors in chapter 2 when he talked about a building growing (v. 21), so he does here. And he certainly does this purposely, to remind us that the Church of Jesus Christ is both a body and a building, and that it must both grow and be built. Neither image is complete in itself.

The body of Christ is to be built up spiritually. A physical body is built up when all its muscles are functioning properly; the Church becomes strong when all its members are performing their ministries. A strong church is an active church. No church can be built up when only a small minority of its membership functions.

But the body of Christ is also to be built up numerically. Naturally, one cannot judge the quality of a church by counting the number of people who attend its services. On the other hand, it is doubtful that any church can grow spiritually without seeing an accompanying growth in numbers.

2. The goal of the ministry (v. 13). The immediate purpose of the ministries is to equip the saints for service. The ultimate goal of the ministry is maturity: maturity in the collective sense, showing itself in united churches; maturity in the individual sense, showing itself in the perfection of Christians. This goal concerns the entire membership of the body of Christ, as is seen in the opening words, "Till we *all* come." Those who are in the ministry must continue to serve until this goal is realized.

The unity of the Church. Chapter 4 begins with unity, then speaks of diversity, and now returns to unity. The unity of the universal Church is based on its uniqueness. However, unity in local churches is a result of their ministry. The spiritual unity of the invisible Church is to be made a visible and practical reality through the faithfulness of those whom our Lord has given to serve it.

This unity is to express itself in two areas: the faith, and the knowledge of the Son of God. The unity of the faith does not mean that all the members of the church should believe the same things, but that they should be united in their response to what they believe. In giving the disciples their commission, Jesus did not say they were to teach all things

He had taught; rather, they were to teach men to observe all these things. God's ministers are to fill men's hearts with motivation to respond to the knowledge they have.

Further, the unity of the knowledge of the Son of God does not simply mean that all the members are to profess the same Christ. It means that they are to be united in their experience of this living Christ, so that they can grow up in Him and so that out of Him the whole body can increase. This is the kind of knowledge Paul spoke of when he exclaimed, "That I may know him, and the power of his resurrection, and the fellowship of his sufferings!" (Phil. 3:10).

This unity is not achieved merely by faithfully preaching the Word. It is a result of equipping the saints for service. The united church is the active church. Some churches are orthodox to the core, but dead, and death always results in disintegration. Is yours a divided church? Perhaps its members have been soaking up truth for years but have not been trained for service. Simply dealing with problems may only tend to exaggerate them. Real solutions lie in a rediscovery of the purpose of the ministry.

The perfection of Christians. "For the perfecting of the saints . . . unto a perfect man." The word used for "perfect" comes from a term sometimes translated "goal." We usually think that the perfect man is the one who has attained his goal. However, Paul's use of the term in Philippians 3:12-14 is different. There he says, "Not as though I had already attained, either were already perfect . . . but . . . I press toward the mark." Then he says in verse 15, "Let us therefore, as many as be perfect, be thus minded." Those who are perfect are those who press toward the mark.

Perfection is not therefore reaching a goal, but reaching toward it. The "perfect" man is the one who is consciously goal-oriented. And his goal is Jesus Christ, in whom all aspects of life find their integration point.

We tend to measure ourselves by standards we have set or by comparing ourselves with others. The measure of Christian perfection, however, is "the measure of the stature of the fulness of Christ." When we press toward the goal of knowing Him, He fills us and pulls together the disintegrated areas of our lives.

3. The results of the ministry (vv. 14-15). The purpose of the ministry is to train saints. The goal of the ministry is maturity, seen in the unity of the Church and the perfection of the Christian. The results of the ministry are now stated in three parts.

"**That we henceforth be no more children.**" One of the marks of immaturity is lack of stability. A child is easily influenced, because he lacks the discernment which comes from having well-defined goals in life. When God's ministers properly perform their functions, one of the results will be Christians who are no longer "tossed to and fro, and carried about with every wind of doctrine." The image is that of a boat which, instead of moving steadily toward its destination, is blown aside by each changing wind.

The importance of spiritual maturity is seen in the latter part of verse 14. Each Christian is subject not only to truth but also to error, and to lead men into error many are willing to use "sleight" and "cunning craftiness." The word translated "sleight" is borrowed from dice-playing; "craftiness" denotes a willingness to do anything in order to deceive. The phrase "whereby they lie in wait to deceive" could be translated, "with a view to the systematizing of error." Not only do the enemies of truth seek to lead into error; they also seek to build error into a system which will effectively enslave the minds of those who are blown off course.

"**Speaking the truth in love.**" Truth is not simply doctrine; it is doctrine that grows out of Christ as He is revealed in the Word. Jesus Christ is the source of all truth, for He is Himself the truth. But Jesus is more than truth; He is also love. His love was so great that He was willing to die for those who hated Him. Therefore, if we really understand what truth and love are, there can be no conflict between the two, for they proceed from the same source.

One of the results of the ministries in the Church is Christians who speak the truth in love. This is not simply to present truth in a pleasing or tactful manner. It is to be truthful, not only in what we say but also in the way we live, because of our love for others.

That we "**may grow up into him in all things.**" Just as perfection goes on to greater perfection, so mature Christians continue to grow. The growth of the body of Christ never ceases; moreover, the more the Church grows spiritually, the greater becomes its capacity for growth. When the Church's ministries are properly functioning, there will be church growth—not simply more people coming out to the services, but "all things" coming to an ever-increasing spiritual maturity.

All growth is in relation to the head, Christ. He is not only the object of our faith; He is also the source of our life.

III. A GROWING CHURCH (4:16)

When God's ministers can faithfully perform their ministries, the Church will be "fitly joined together and compacted by that which every joint supplieth," and it will grow. Verse 16 forms a fitting summary to this passage; it is a remarkable statement.

1. Christ is the source of Church growth. A healthy church is a growing church. In verse 16 Paul uses two terms to indicate growth: "increase of the body" and "edifying." The first indicates growth of the Church as Christ's body. The second indicates growth of the Church as a building. Church growth is to be both spiritual and numerical. The Church grows spiritually when each member increases in maturity; it grows numerically when new stones are added to the structure.

All true growth, whether spiritual or numerical, comes out of Christ, who is the head. We talk a lot about church growth and about ways to make a church grow. We can learn much from these discussions, for many excellent suggestions have been offered to help churches achieve normal growth. Some growth, however, is artificial, the result of methods which could be applied to any kind of organization. All true growth, regardless of the methods used, can only come out of Christ, "the fulness of him that filleth all in all."

2. To grow, the Church must be "fitly joined together and compacted." Just as Paul uses two terms to speak of growth, so he uses two terms to indicate the condition for growth. "Fitly joined together" is the same term he used in 2:21; it refers to a building which is properly framed. "Compacted" refers to a body knit together by sinews, ligaments, and joints.

Most of us realize that a growing church must also be united internally. The Church is not a monstrosity in which each member grows directly out of the head; the members are put in a body which allows them to function properly. The Church is also a building in which each stone has a relationship with other stones, as well as with the cornerstone.

Therefore, in the Church the "joints" play an indispensable part; these "joints," it would seem, are the ministers that Jesus Christ gives His body in order for it to function properly. Unless a church is structured, it is not a true representation of the body of Christ. Church growth implies a functioning ministry.

When the joints are functioning, each member can play its part. The phrases, "according to the effectual working in the measure of every part," could be translated "when each part is working properly," and simply indicates that in a healthy body each member does what it is supposed to do, with the cooperation of the entire body.

3. Growth can only be "in love." Why do some churches fail to grow even when everything is apparently well organized and functioning properly? The answer might be found in the last two words of verse 16, "in love." Love is one of the things that holds the body together and makes real growth possible. Where there is no love, the pastor might speak with the tongues of men and angels and the people might have all knowledge and faith, but to no avail. Love results in loyalty, and without the loyalty that every closely knit family knows, even the most clever methods end in discouragement. If a church is filled with suspicion and criticism, it cannot be a growing church, either spiritually or numerically. At the beginning of Ephesians 4 the Apostle exhorts the Ephesians to forbear one another in love. It is when this climate of love is created that the body will grow normally.

It was said of the early Christians, "Behold, how they love one another!" What do people say about your church?

Questions for Discussion

1. What is the difference between "gifts," "administrations," and "operations"?

2. Can a pastor be subject to a church board and still be free to exercise his spiritual authority?

3. What practical steps can your church take to improve the training of members?

4. What are the marks of Christian maturity?

5. Can a church retain doctrinal purity and still show love? Is there a conflict between the two?

6. How can church growth be measured?

9

Putting Off the Old Man

EPHESIANS 4:17-32

THE CHAPTER OUTLINED:

I. **The Walk of the Gentiles**
1. The mind of the Gentiles
2. The faith of the Gentiles
3. The morality of the Gentiles

II. **The Old Man and the New**
1. Put off the old man
2. "Put on the new man"
3. "Be renewed in the spirit of your mind"

III. **Four Commands**
1. Lying
2. Anger
3. Stealing
4. Speech

IV. **"Grieve Not the Holy Spirit"**

The letter to the Ephesians is in two parts. The first part is mainly doctrinal and reveals our calling. The second part is practical and concerns our walk. As new men we are to walk in a manner worthy of our vocation.

We have been called both out of this world and into the Church. Therefore, in our walk we must both refuse the life-style we formerly knew when we "walked according to the course of this world," and accept a new way of life which is in conformity with our relationship with Christ and our spiritual brothers. The first part of chapter 4 offers some general principles regarding our walk in the Church. Now we shall study specific commands that reveal the contrast between the "new man" and the life he formerly knew.

This section of Ephesians covers 4:17 to 5:21; we shall divide it into two parts for our study. The first part seems to emphasize the negative aspects of the Christian's walk, spelling out what he must no longer do. It begins with the words, "Walk not as other Gentiles walk," and its key verse is "Grieve not the holy Spirit." The second part (which we shall study in the next chapter) puts more emphasis on the positive side. It begins with the command, "Walk in love," and its key verse is, "Be filled with the Spirit." Naturally, however, one cannot completely separate the positive aspects of our walk from the negatives, and so throughout this passage we shall find a mixture of both.

I. THE WALK OF THE GENTILES (4:17-19)

The Apostle has just revealed that the Church is a marvelous body in which every member has a unique role to play. Then immediately he states, "This I say therefore, and testify in the Lord, that ye henceforth walk not as other Gentiles walk." The command is forceful; as members of Christ's body we have no right to continue the kind of life we knew before our conversion.

The term "Gentiles" translates the word for "nations" and refers to those whom Paul said were formerly "without Christ, being aliens from the commonwealth of Israel, and strangers from the covenants of promise, having no hope, and without God in the world" (2:12). The word is used in its spiritual sense, referring to the unsaved man, who walks according to the world and its prince and who is dominated by the flesh and its desires.

How, then, do the Gentiles walk? The Apostle exposes their life-style in three areas: thoughts, belief, and morals.

1. The mind of the Gentiles (vv. 17-18). Actions always proceed from thoughts; to understand why someone acts a certain way, we must penetrate his mind and try to determine how he thinks. Therefore, before getting into specifics about the walk of the Gentiles, Paul peers into their thinking processes. He tells us two things.

First, he reveals that the unsaved walk according to the "vanity" of their minds. The word "vanity" does not mean pride; it rather carries the idea of purposelessness, or aimlessness. We saw in our last study that the perfect man is the man who lives according to goals. True spirituality means living above the immediate, being willing to sift the various thoughts that come through our consciousness and react only to those which lead us to a greater conformity to Christ. However, the Gentile's thinking is aimless; whatever crosses his mind becomes the motivation for his actions.

Second, Paul reveals that the understanding of the unsaved man is darkened. For the Christians he prayed that the eyes of their understanding might be enlightened in order that they might perceive spiritual truth. But the understanding of the Gentiles is like a dark closet, having no windows, and closed off from the light of God by a door bolted by unbelief.

2. The faith of the Gentiles (v. 18). Why is their understanding darkened? Because they are alienated from the life of God. God is light; apart from Him all is in darkness. Paul traces man's alienation from God to two causes. The first is ignorance; the second is hardness (which is the correct translation of the word "blindness"). These two always go together. In Romans 1:20-32 the Apostle states plainly that men are without excuse, "because that, when they knew God, they glorified him not as God. . . . And even as they did not like to retain God in their knowledge, God gave them over to a reprobate mind" (vv. 21, 28).

It is true that many people have intellectual problems concerning God. In nearly every case, however, these intellectual problems are the result of hearts that have become hardened. "If any man will do his will," said Jesus, "he shall know the doctrine, whether it be of God, or whether I speak of myself" (John 7:17).

3. The morality of the Gentiles (v. 19). Rejection of God leads to darkened minds, but it does not stop there; it results in depraved lives. Just as God gave men up to reprobate minds, so He gave them over to vile affections (Rom. 1:26). The man whom the Bible calls a fool not only says in his heart that there is no God; he also is corrupt in his life (see Ps.

14:1-3). No man can reject God, the source of all that is good, and retain a life of moral purity.

The unsaved are here described as being "past feeling." Their consciences are seared to the point where they no longer feel pain from wrongdoing. Because of this, they can devote themselves fully to "lasciviousness," which means moral license. Further, they do this with "greediness," for formal sin continually craves more and is never satisfied.

II. THE OLD MAN AND THE NEW (4:20-24)

"But ye have not so learned Christ." The contrast between verses 19 and 20 is emphatic; so must be the contrast between the life-style of Gentiles and that of believers. The word "learn" brings to mind a disciple, one who learns both by hearing his master's teaching and by following his example.

The believers had "learned" Christ by hearing Him through the preaching of the apostles. Though it is doubtful that they themselves had heard the Lord personally, they had seen Him in the lives of men who had been transformed by knowing Him.

Further, they had "been taught," and this teaching was in conformity with the truth that is in Jesus. For them, Jesus was not just a name, as is true for so many who claim to have accepted Him but whose experience is little more than emotional. Their faith had doctrinal content. Jesus is a person who is real, and our salvation depends upon what He really did. To know Him means to accept the doctrinal truths of the incarnation, atonement, and resurrection, and to apply these truths to our lives.

A part of the truth they had learned is expressed in three phrases, found in verses 22 to 24: "put off," "be renewed," and "put on."

1. **Put off the old man (v. 22).** The image of the old and new man is a favorite of Paul's. In Romans 6:6 he states that our old man has been crucified with Christ. This refers to our regeneration. In Colossians 3:9 and 10 he says that we have already put off the old man and put on the new. This refers to our conversion. Here in Ephesians he indicates that the believer is to continue to put off the old man and put on the new. This refers to our consecration. In other words, we are to translate into our walk the truth of our identification with Christ.

Christians are sometimes confused about the old man. The old man is not the old nature. The old nature does not die when we accept Christ. Nor can we put it off, as we would remove a garment; it remains with us until we are made perfectly whole by the presence of the Lord. The old man is the man who is enslaved by his sinful nature; the new man is the one who has been liberated because Christ rules in his heart.

To put off the old man is to refuse our "former conversation," which means our former manner of life. Though our old man legally died at our conversion, and though our sinful nature no longer has authority to enslave us, we can still choose to submit to its domination. Two kinds of life are open to us: life in the flesh, or life in the Spirit.

The dominant characteristic of the old man is corruption. When the first man sinned, he died, and this death produced both physical and spiritual disintegration. To allow oneself to be dominated by the sinful nature is to hasten this process of disintegration. "To be carnally minded is death; but to be spiritually minded is life and peace" (Rom. 8:6).

How do we put off the old man? The verb form in the original indicates action that is decisive. The Christian is not to waste his time trying to decide which suit to wear; his clothing is to fit his transformed personality, and if at any point he realizes that Christ is no longer on the throne, he is to "put off" once and for all the life-style in which he is dominated by his carnal nature.

2. "Put on the new man" (v. 24). If the old man is the man who lives under the control of sin, the new man is the one who lives under the control of Christ through the Holy Spirit. The old man has been crucified with Christ. The new man shares His resurrection. "If any man be in Christ, he is a new creature" (II Cor. 5:17).

Just as we are to put off the old man in actual practice, so are we to put on the new. How do we do this? Simply by allowing Christ to rule. "Walk in the Spirit, and ye shall not fulfil the lust of the flesh" (Gal. 5:16). As new creatures we have a new nature, for when we accepted Christ, our bodies became the temple of the Holy Spirit. His presence breaks the authority of our sinful nature and provides the power we need both to defeat sin and to produce spiritual fruit. The power, however, is effective only when we choose it. Just as someone must throw a switch to allow the power of electricity to flow through a house, so must we, by a decision of the will, consciously submit the control of our lives to Him.

Putting on the new man must be an experience as decisive as putting off the old. If we are living defeated lives it is not because God's power is insufficient, or because we are special cases, or because our wills are too weak. It is because of indecision. The remedy for indecision is not prayer, counseling, or a deeper understanding of the Scriptures. It is decision.

Power always follows purpose.

Just as the dominant characteristic of the old man is corruption, that of the new man is creation. The new man is the one who, in the likeness of God, "is created in righteousness and true holiness." Righteousness and holiness refer to the two aspects of our sanctification; we are to be righteous in our relation to God, and holy in our relation to sin.

The creative power of the new man puts back together what sin has disintegrated. God's goal for us is that we become completely integrated persons under the total authority of Christ. This creation, this new man, is the result of the direct intervention of God's Spirit in our personalities. It began at the time of our regeneration, when God's Spirit united with ours, and it continues as we submit our broken beings to Him.

3. "Be renewed in the spirit of your mind" (v. 23). The third command which forms a part of the teaching of the Ephesian Christians is sandwiched between the two others, and for a reason. It is a result of both and cannot be separated from either. One cannot put on the new man without putting off the old, nor can he put off the old without putting on the new. Like exhaling and inhaling, they are two sides of the same experience. And just as breathing brings renewal to the body, so we are spiritually renewed when Christ rules.

The other two commands designate a decisive action; this one indicates a continuing process. When we refuse the sinful nature and submit to the Spirit, our own spirits experience continual renewal. Paul talks about this renewal in II Corinthians 4:16: "Though our outward man perish, yet the inward man is renewed day by day." Our bodies wear out; their complete renewal must await the Resurrection. But their spiritual renewal has already begun.

Paul says that this renewal is in "the spirit of your mind." By this he means that it is in the consciousness. He expresses the same truth in Romans 12:1-2, where he exhorts us to present our bodies to God (putting on the new man), to refuse to conform ourselves to this world (putting off the old), and to be transformed "by the renewing of your mind." It is in our mind that God's Spirit unites with ours. To be sure, we are not usually consciously aware of what the Holy Spirit is doing. "The wind bloweth where it listeth, and thou hearest the sound thereof, but canst not tell whence it cometh, and whither it goeth" (John 3:8). But on the other hand, He cannot renew us unless we consciously open our minds to His influence.

III. FOUR COMMANDS (4:25-29)

So that none of his readers will misunderstand what he means by putting off the old man, Paul spells it out in four specific commands. There is no contradiction between the great truth of our identification with Christ on the one hand, and precise instruction about Christian conduct on the other. For some, commands seem superfluous; they are able to grasp quickly the practical implications of being crucified with Christ. Others understand better when things are stated more specifically. But whether one approaches the Christian walk from the side of general principles or specific orders, he is to arrive at obedience. Anyone who pretends to have a special understanding of the deeper life without obeying God's commands is only deceiving himself.

The four commands listed by Paul concern sins which were common among the Gentiles—and are just as common today. They are stated in the negative, but each is accompanied by an exhortation for positive Christian conduct.

1. Lying (v. 25). Of the seven things God hates (Prov. 6:16-19), lying is mentioned twice. Perhaps it is because lying is a willful disintegration of the personality, a direct violation of what the Holy Spirit is attempting to do in us. Jesus Christ is not only the way and the life; He is also the truth. To lie is to deny Him in our conduct. Lying is one of the most "spiritual" of the sins common to man, for men usually do not lie because of the passions of their sinful nature, but because of a willful desire to deceive.

Putting off the old man means putting off lying; putting on the new means speaking the truth. Just as lying is a willful act, so speaking the truth must be willful. It is possible to deceive by remaining silent when we should speak. The Christian should be willing to be truthful with others, even when it is difficult.

The reason for speaking the truth is that we are members of one another. The Church grows when all its members are properly joined together, "compacted by that which every joint supplieth." If lying results in a disintegration of the personality, it has the same effect in the Church.

2. Anger (vv. 26-27). Paul's statement about anger is most interesting because it implies a difference between anger which is sin and that which is not. All of us feel anger when things cross us; not to be able to feel anger is to be less than human on the level of emotional response. However, it is one thing to feel anger and another to yield to it. When we are angry, we are faced with the choice of either dominating our feelings through the

Holy Spirit, or of being dominated by them. To put off the old man is to refuse to be enslaved by our feelings.

We should not let the sun go down on our wrath. Before the end of the day, we are to deal spiritually with carnal feelings, so that we can know the peace of God which allows us the rest we need. It is interesting that the latter part of the verse Paul quotes, Psalm 4:4, continues, "Commune with your own heart upon your bed, and be still." When we sleep, we have little control over the unconscious part of our mind, which is the seat of our sinful nature. Therefore, we must be in communion with God before drifting into unconsciousness. To go to sleep with bitter feelings smouldering in our hearts is to "give place to the devil" (Eph. 4:27).

3. Stealing (v. 28). One would think that it not be necessary for Paul to warn his converts against stealing; yet, this was so much a way of life for some that they would find it quite natural to continue, especially when stealing apparently did no harm, as would be true when a slave stole from his master. The command, however, is rigid. There is to be no stealing of any kind. And when one remembers that most of the stealing in stores today is done by the employees, he realizes that our situation is similiar to that of Paul's day.

In nearly every culture certain forms of stealing are condemned by society, whereas others are tolerated. Few have pangs of conscience about stealing from the government by falsifying tax returns. Employees steal not only by actually taking things, but also by failing to give an honest day's work. Students steal by cheating on their exams. In fact, whole political movements are based on the premise that it is right to steal from the rich in order to give to the poor.

If putting off the old man means to refuse all forms of stealing, putting on the new man means to work, not only to satisfy our own needs, but also to be able to give to others so that they will not be tempted to steal.

4. Speech (v. 29). Paul states that the Christian's speech should always be "seasoned with salt" (Col. 4:6). Since salt was used mainly as a preservative in ancient times, we can assume that he meant our speech should be infused with the kind of positive thinking that would keep it from becoming corrupt, or rotten. Words that are corrupt are also corrupting, just as a rotten apple will eventually spoil the whole lot. One cannot hear some people talk without feeling dirty; the believer, in putting off the old man, must refuse the degrading speech patterns of the world.

If the tongue can be an instrument for evil, it is also a powerful instrument for good. What a blessing it is to be in the company of God's children who use their words to build up, ministering grace to their hearers! This, too, is a part of the walk of the Christian who "puts on" the new man.

IV. "GRIEVE NOT THE HOLY SPIRIT" (4:30-32)

There is really no break in thought between verses 29 and 30. To indulge in degrading conversation is to grieve the Holy Spirit and prevent the edification of the body of Christ. However, this statement forms a fitting conclusion to the entire section from verses 17 through 32, for the Christian walk is in the Spirit, and to grieve Him is to make Christianity an empty performance.

The Book of Ephesians emphasizes repeatedly that the Holy Spirit is our source of spiritual power. We must never think, however, that this power is impersonal. The Holy Spirit can be quenched through neglect or prayer and God's Word; He can also be grieved by conduct which is unbecoming for the child of God.

To grieve the Spirit does not mean to lose Him, for by Him we are "sealed unto the day of redemption." We need not fear for our eternal salvation; we need rather fear that by conduct which is not worthy of our Lord we shall deny ourselves the sheer joy of intimate fellowship with Him. A wife who grieves her husband is not necessarily inviting divorce; she is denying herself the blessings of the marriage relationship.

"The fruit of the Spirit is love, joy, peace, longsuffering, gentleness, goodness, faith, meekness, temperance" (Gal. 5:22-23). These are not only qualities that He wants to produce in us; they are also, in a sense, marks of His own personality. To grieve the Holy Spirit is to engage in conduct that is in conflict with what He is, and what He wants to produce in us.

The Holy Spirit dwells in all members of Christ's body; He is not our private possession. Bitterness, wrath, and anger are sins against our brothers in Christ; to strike out against a brother is to hurt the Holy Spirit, for He loves our brother as much as He loves us. We must put away clamor, evil speaking, and malice if we wish to see the body edified in love.

Therefore, says the Apostle, "Be ye kind one to another, tenderhearted." Being new men means assuming new attitudes, attitudes which allow God's Spirit to move freely among us. For if He is a person who can be grieved, He is also a person who can be pleased. We must express our attitudes in action: "forgiving one another, even as God for Christ's sake hath forgiven you." To be kind and tenderhearted means more than having a gentle personality; it means being willing to ask forgiveness, and to forgive, just as our Lord forgave us.

Are you in a church where the Holy Spirit has been grieved, so that there is no longer any thrill in coming together? Perhaps healing will have to start at the place where this study ends—"forgiving one another." If there are hurts in the past, it will do little good to try to determine who was right or who was wrong. Four simple words, "Will you forgive me," could be enough to open a door that would release the bitterness that has been penned up for years.

Questions for Discussion

1. Do you feel that conduct is always the result of belief? Can a man live a life of good morals without believing in God?

2. Why do you think the teaching of our being crucified with Christ has led some Christians to a false spirituality?

3. Why does Paul put so much emphasis on the mind in his teaching about the Christian life?

4. Among your Christian friends are you conscious of double standards with respect to the four sins listed in this study: lying, anger, stealing, and bad language?

5. How can we tell when the Holy Spirit is grieved in our churches?

6. Do you think that kindness is mainly a personality trait, or an attitude?

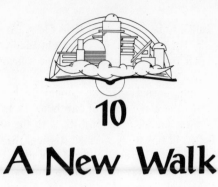

10

A New Walk

EPHESIANS 5:1-21

THE CHAPTER OUTLINED:

I. Walking in Love
  1. True love
  2. Counterfeit love

II. Walking in Light
  1. The fruit of light
  2. Light and discernment
  3. "Awake thou that sleepest"

III. Walking in Wisdom
  1. Redeeming the time
  2. Understanding the will of the Lord

IV. "Be Filled with the Spirit"
  1. Praise
  2. Giving thanks
  3. Submission

We have been called to be new men in Jesus Christ. As new men, we are to have a new walk. The early believers called Christianity "the way"; it is natural therefore that the term "walk" should be a favorite with Paul to designate our Christian experience.

Our last study emphasized that we should no longer walk as the Gentiles, according to the aimlessness of our thoughts. Lying, anger, stealing, filthy speech—these are all to be put off, with the old man, for they grieve the Holy Spirit. In this study we shall consider the Christian walk in some of its positive aspects. Here we are told to walk in love, in light, and in wisdom. As in our last study the negative aspects of our walk were balanced by positive exhortations, so here the Apostle emphasizes the positive features of our walk by contrasting them with negatives.

Walking is a skill. One of a child's first major hurdles is to learn to walk, and it is something which costs hours of practice, plus many bruises. Walking requires effort. It makes us get up and move and causes us to breathe deeply. Walking is necessary for the body to maintain its strength. Many physical problems are solved when people begin to walk regularly.

Too many Christians fail to see their spiritual life as a walk. They are "resting in the Lord" with too much ease. Perhaps this study will help us get rid of an easy-chair mentality and start moving. Spiritual problems are often caused by inactivity. "Wherefore lift up the hands which hang down, and the feeble knees; and make straight paths for your feet, lest that which is lame be turned out of the way; but let it rather be healed" (Heb. 12:12-13). Walking brings healing.

I. WALKING IN LOVE (5:1-7)

As God's children how should we walk? The answer is to be His followers. The word "follower" translates a word from which we get "mimic." Being a follower of God means to imitate Him. All children begin their learning process by imitating. Imitating does not require reflection; a child imitates simply by copying what he sees.

Of course, we cannot see our Heavenly Father, and so we must imitate Christ. "No man hath seen God at any time; the only begotten Son, which is in the bosom of the Father, he hath declared him" (John 1:18). When we imitate Christ, we see that the dominant feature of His life was love. We are therefore to walk in love.

1. True love (vv. 1-2). The word "love" is used in three ways in the first two verses: as an adjective, as a noun, and as a verb.

As children of God we are loved. (The word "dear" in verse 1 translates "beloved.") Love is the most important element in training a child. No child can develop normally without it. We learn to love by experiencing love from others. "We love him, because he first loved us" (I John 4:19).

As children of God we are to walk in love. Love provides the context for our Christian walk. It is to be our basic attitude toward God and our fellow man. The word used for "love" is *agape,* which is not love in the sense of liking or generating warm feelings. Rather, it is an attitude which results from choice. To love others is to desire their best.

As children of God we are to follow the example of Christ, who loved. Verse 2 is an outstanding expression of Christ's love. First, it tells us that His love gave. Love always expresses itself in action. Because God loved, He gave. Second, verse 2 points out the fact that Jesus' love was sacrificial. We shall never fully fathom the depth of this love which was so great that it caused the eternal Son to assume the form of humanity, identify with the sins of man, and die on the cross. Third, we learn that Jesus' love purifies. Paul states specifically that Christ gave himself "for us." His sacrifice made it possible for us to be made holy and without blame. Finally, the verse points out that Jesus' love satisfies. He gave himself as "a sacrifice to God for a sweet-smelling savour." These terms refer to the Temple sacrifices, which brought satisfaction to God and restored fellowship with His people. True love is satisfying love which unites the spirits of those who love.

2. Counterfeit love (vv. 3-7). Most commentators put these verses in a separate category; for this study we shall see them rather as a contrast to the pure love of Christ. True love is not attainable by the world; in fact, the word *agape* is practically nonexistent in ancient secular literature. It is only natural, therefore, that the world should seek a substitute for what it cannot attain. That substitute is lust.

Though lust is termed love in the degraded language of the world, it is the total opposite of genuine love. True love gives; lust covets. True love sacrifices itself; lust sacrifices others. True love purifies; lust degrades. True love satisfies; lust leaves a gnawing emptiness.

In these verses Paul condemns moral impurity in three areas of human experience: acts, language, and thoughts.

Impure acts (v. 3). The Apostle chooses three terms to describe impurity. The first, "fornication," refers to unlawful sexual intercourse. The second, "uncleanness," broadens the reference to all forms of moral impurity, including those which are contrary to nature. The third, "covetousness," can refer to any kind of unlawful desire, but it is here associated with unrestraint in sexual passion.

These things must not even be named among Christians. This does not mean that they should not be talked about, for Paul mentions them frequently in his letter, but rather that the Christian's reputation should not be tainted by moral impurity. God's children are saints; they are to be entirely dedicated to Him.

Impure language (v. 4). Many people who would not engage bodily in acts of impurity are nevertheless defiled in their language. Paul condemns bad language as being improper for those who walk in love. The tongue can be a powerful instrument for good, but it can also spread corruption. Just as Paul chose three words to describe impurity in acts, he adds three more to refer to impurity in language. "Filthiness" refers to obscene speech. "Foolish talking" doubtless means flippant talking about sexual things. "Jesting" refers to off-color jokes poking fun at the sins of others.

These words certainly do not condemn good humor. "A merry heart doeth good like a medicine" (Prov. 17:22). Though good humor is uplifting, however, filthy stories degrade. In one sense, to make sexual sin the object of jokes is almost worse than the sin itself, for it is to make mockery of God's law.

The tongue is not to remain silent, though; it is to be used for giving thanks. Paul develops this thought more fully in verses 18 to 21.

Impure hearts (v. 5). Impure acts and impure language are an expression of impure hearts. Jesus said clearly that it is from the heart of man that proceed "evil thoughts, adulteries, fornications, murders, thefts, covetousness, wickedness, deceit, lasciviousness, an evil eye, blasphemy, pride, foolishness" (Mark 7:21-22). For this reason, Paul pries deeper in his condemnation of false love, stating that no one who is sexually impure in his heart can hope to inherit the kingdom of Christ and of God.

Paul is not just talking about a person who has sinful thoughts, as is evident by his inclusion of the word "idolater." He is referring to people who have made sex their God and who are worshiping it in their hearts just as other men worship their Creator. As love is an attitude of the heart, so is lust. God's grace forgives all sins, including sexual sins, but it can do nothing for the man who purposes in his heart to bow down to the gods of impurity.

A solemn warning (vv. 6-7). There were many deceivers in the churches of Paul's time. Some of them, strongly influenced by pagan philosophies, pretended that no physical act could harm the spirit, so that the believer could continue to indulge in sexual promiscuity while retaining his purity before God. Further, some Christians, perverting the truth of God's grace, taught that sin only caused His grace to abound.

In our day as well, churches have been infiltrated with deceivers who pretend that true love allows us to live above the rigid sexual code of the Bible. This is usually only a cover for lust. Sex has become the god of this latter half of the twentieth century, and it counts as its worshipers many professing Christians.

Let us not be deceived by empty words. God's standards have not changed, and neither should ours. Though we cannot always understand the reason for the rigidity of the moral laws, may we be willing to believe that God knows man better than he knows himself, and that these laws, rather than limiting him, can enable man to become free and live a fulfilled life. Sexual perversion calls down God's wrath. Those who walk in love are not to be "partakers" of the immorality of their times.

II. WALKING IN LIGHT (5:8-14)

God is light; all else is darkness. But just as the moon reflects the light of the sun, so the believer reflects the light of God. Therefore, Paul states that we, who were darkness, are now light in the Lord and that we should walk as children of light.

Love gives the Christian walk its motivation; light provides discernment. It is impossible to walk in darkness without stumbling over things that clutter the way. Walking in light, we see clearly where we should go.

1. The fruit of light (v. 9). A better reading for "fruit of the Spirit" is "fruit of the light." To be sure, it is the Spirit who produces fruit, as we see in Paul's statement in Galatians 5:22. But light is also necessary, in that it provides the right situation for the Holy Spirit to act freely. Unless plants are placed in the light, sap does not bring life into their cells.

This verse does not say the fruit of the light *is* goodness, righteousness, and truth. We understand this to mean that walking in light is synonymous here with practicing goodness, righteousness, and truth, and that this kind of conduct provides the climate in which spiritual fruit grows.

It is a shame that we are not always transparent in our relationships with others. To walk in goodness, righteousness, and truth is to be above-board, frank, and candid. How often problems could be avoided if these qualities were practiced!

2. Light and discernment (vv. 10-13). Walking as children of light is a condition for discernment. Paul prayed that the Philippian Christians might "approve things that are excellent" (Phil. 1:10). The same thought appears here. When one is in the light, he can see clearly enough to distinguish between good and evil. To walk in darkness is to reduce everything to a state of moral relativity.

Discernment means "*proving* what is acceptable unto the Lord." To prove is to examine. It is to test by applying certain criteria. The word "agreeable" means "well-pleasing."

Discernment also means "reproving" the "unfruitful works of darkness." Light produces fruit; darkness produces only unfruitful works. The fruit of the Spirit contains the power of reproduction, it is creative. But the works of darkness are dead and unfruitful.

How are the children of the light to reprove the works of darkness? Not by discussion. "It is a shame even to speak of those things which are done by them in secret" (v. 12). The works of darkness are so degrading that the Christian is to avoid filling his mind with them. Immorality is not to be the topic of discussion for those who know God, any more than it is to be the subject of jesting for those who do not.

Rather, "all things that are reproved are made manifest by the light" (v. 13). Have you ever thrown open the shutters of a room on a bright sunny day, revealing all the dust and cobwebs that had been collecting for weeks in the darkness? The Christian who is willing to walk as a child of light has much the same effect on the works of darkness. He is light; light and darkness cannot coexist. Just as spiritual fruit needs light, sin needs darkness. "Ye are the light of the world," said Jesus. "A city that is set on an hill cannot be hid. . . . Let your light so shine before men, that they may see your good works, and glorify your Father which is in heaven" (Matt. 5:14, 16).

3. "Awake thou that sleepest" (v. 14). This verse is obviously a quotation, but its source is not identified. Some have suggested that it was taken from an ancient hymn used at baptisms. Whatever its origin, it forms a fitting conclusion to this passage on light, for before walking, one must wake up. Light may be streaming through the windows, but the sleeper is unaware that it is morning. To awaken to Christ is compared to arising from the dead.

Christ is for us an unquenchable source of light. He is the light that shines in darkness, and the darkness cannot put it out (John 1:5). For all who are willing to awaken to Him, His light is sufficient.

III. WALKING IN WISDOM (5:15-16)

Walking in love provides motivation; walking in light allows discernment; walking in wisdom leads to right decisions. Love, light, and wisdom cannot be separated. "God hath not given us the spirit of fear; but of power, and of love, and of a sound mind" (II Tim. 1:7).

The word "circumspectly" means accurately, or with care. Light reveals the way we should go; wisdom means going in that way. We can excuse someone for falling into a ditch in the darkness; to fall into it in broad daylight is the mark of a fool.

God's grace has been given to His children "in all wisdom and prudence," allowing them to know "the mystery of his will" (1:8-9). Paul has already prayed that the Ephesians might have "the spirit of wisdom" in their knowledge of Him. Now he commands them to walk in that wisdom.

1. Redeeming the time (v. 16). Walking in wisdom implies two things: first, redeeming the time, and second, understanding God's will.

To redeem the time is to make the necessary sacrifice in order to take advantage of opportunity when it presents itself. Wise King Solomon said there was a time for everything, and the wise Christian will heed this statement. When things are done in their time, they are usually easy. When that time passes, simple neglect brings complications and even tragedy. A surgeon who fails to perform the simple act of washing his hands before an operation can bring weeks of suffering or even death, in spite of his great skill. He can wash all he likes afterward, but the damage is already done. The "time" has passed.

To walk wisely is to be willing to structure our time and discipline ourselves according to that structure. It is no mark of spirituality to react to the impulse of the moment. We live in time; time is a necessary factor in everything we do. No amount of consecration or good intentions can make up for sloppy planning and laziness. A Christian can be superbly gifted, but if he is not willing to "redeem the time," his very gifts become a source of depression. Without doubt, the greatest waste in the Church is the waste of believers' time. When the "time" to do something passes, no amount of money or effort can buy it back.

We should redeem the time "because the days are evil." In Paul's day, persecution threatened the Church; in ours, impending judgment. At best, the world can continue in its present course for only a few generations. When he wrote to the Colossians, Paul told them to redeem the time in their witness to others (Col. 4:5). While the majority of the world's population still lies in darkness, we must seize the opportunity to share the good news.

2. Understanding the will of the Lord (v. 17). God's great will as the supreme Administrator of the universe is to bring all things under Christ's authority. We have a part to play in this plan; walking in wisdom means "understanding what the will of the Lord is" in our particular walk.

The word "understanding" means gaining insight; the Scriptures often associate understanding with knowing God's will. In Psalm 32 we find the promise that God will instruct us and teach us in the way we should go. Then immediately we are warned not to be like a horse or mule, "which have no understanding."

The thing which distinguishes men from beasts in their walk is understanding. Dumb beasts must be kept in line with bit and bridle; men are to walk with understanding. Unfortunately, many Christians lower themselves to the level of animals in their search for God's will, by their insistence on signs, open and closed doors, and inner feelings. It is through the renewing of our *mind* that we are enabled to discern the Lord's will (Rom. 12:2).

IV. "BE FILLED WITH THE SPIRIT" (5:18-21)

These verses are not separated from those which precede them; to be filled with the Spirit is one of the aspects of walking in wisdom. However, as was true with the command to "grieve not the holy Spirit" in chapter 4, this command rises above the others and merits special attention, for it summarizes all the others.

Paul states that all Christians have been baptized in the Holy Spirit (I Cor. 12:13). Further, he makes it plain that all Christians are indwelt with the Spirit (Rom. 8:9). But, writing to Christians who are both baptized in the Spirit and indwelt by Him, Paul commands, "Be filled." It is possible to be indwelt with the Spirit without being filled.

Many Christians are perplexed about the Spirit's filling, especially when bombarded with all the conflicting teaching about His ministries. Part of this confusion stems from a misunderstanding of the word "filled." They tend to visualize the Spirit's filling much in the same way as a container would be filled with liquid.

Paul's surprising association of drunkenness and the filling of the Spirit, however, provides us with a clue as to the meaning of this experience. Though drunkenness is the exact opposite of the Spirit's filling in its effects on the person, it is nevertheless similar in its nature. In both drunkenness and the filling of the Spirit, a person's will becomes subject to another force. Through drunkenness his will becomes subject to his lower nature; the filling of the Spirit, however, subjects it to Christ.

To be filled with the Spirit is to be controlled by Him. And because the Holy Spirit renews us in the "spirit of the mind," or the consciousness, the command here is that we submit all that enters our consciousness to His control. Because the verb denotes a continual action, we must continually submit those aspects of our lives that come to our attention, so that He can control us completely, bringing harmony and spiritual power.

Three marks of the Spirit-filled life are listed in the verses that follow.

1. Praise (v. 19). "Speaking to yourselves" should be understood as "speaking to one another." "Psalms, hymns, and spiritual songs" refer to the various types of singing that have characterized Christian worship. As those who walk in darkness are noted for their bawdy songs, Christians are to express their joy to God in the form of music. Singing is one of the finest ways of praising God, for it brings emotions and intelligence together in the melody and words of a song and presents them both to God in worship. Spirit-filled Christians are always known for their joyful singing.

2. Giving thanks (v. 20). Many Christians experience a spiritual revolution in their lives when they begin practicing thankfulness. Spirit-filled Christians are to give thanks "always for all things." In the same way that we are to pray without ceasing, we are to thank God without ceasing. Each new circumstance becomes an occasion for giving thanks.

Thanks is to be for all things. In I Thessalonians 5:18 we have a hint as to how we can thank God even for difficult things. There Paul says, "In every thing give thanks: for this is the will of God in Christ Jesus concerning you." We thank God for misfortunes, not because we are spiritual neurotics, taking pleasure in our woes, but because God is doing everything according to a plan. In His plan even the somber pieces fit together like a jigsaw puzzle to form a perfect picture.

For this reason we offer our thanks to God and the Father in the name of our Lord Jesus Christ. If God were not our Father, and if Jesus Christ were not our Lord, we would have reason to complain. Because God is on

His throne, all things will continue to work together for our eternal good, as He planned from the beginning.

3. Submission (v. 21). The third mark of the Spirit-filled life is submission. As we are to submit to circumstances, so we are to submit to others. God's plan for us includes not only the things that happen, but also the people who cause them to happen.

To submit to one another does not mean to disregard the principle of authority on which God has structured human society. As we shall see in the next study, there is social submission as well as personal. Submission here means rather becoming a servant of all in fearful reverence for Christ. He came not to be served, but to serve, even though He is the King of kings and the Lord of lords. To be filled with the spirit of this world is to try to dominate; to be filled with Christ's Spirit is to become the servant of all.

Walking as new men is being filled with His Spirit, allowing Him to control. When He is really in charge, we begin to see God, circumstances, and others in their true perspective. If the Holy Spirit is really on the throne, we can trust Him to arrange things as He chooses, so that praise, thanksgiving, and submission are merely our normal responses.

Questions for Discussion

1. How can we determine whether our love for our brethren is really *agape* love?

2. When, among Christians, does good humor risk becoming "foolish talking"?

3. What can churches do to stem the tide of moral uncleanness?

4. Does planning one's time limit the Holy Spirit?

5. Do you think that the Christian can become too preoccupied with the Holy Spirit? Explain.

6. Can a normal person really thank God for tragedies?

11

Husbands, Wives
and the Church

EPHESIANS 5:22-33

THE CHAPTER OUTLINED:

I. **Wives and Submission**
   1. Submission is voluntary
   2. "As unto the Lord"
   3. "The husband is the head of the wife"
   4. "In everything"

II. **Husbands and Love**
   1. What love is
   2. What love does

III. **One Flesh**
   1. Marriage constitutes a new body
   2. "Two shall be one flesh"

The first part of the Ephesian letter emphasizes revelation; the latter part, relationships. In chapter 5, verses 22 to 33, we have a wonderful blend of the two, in which the marriage relationship is portrayed against the background of Christ's relationship to His Church.

It is a superb piece of literature, in which the Apostle weaves the two themes together with the skill of an artist. Here we find marriage elevated to its original purity. No one can really know this passage and still insist that Paul had a low view of marriage. That the Church during a long period of its history exalted celibacy is only an indication of its ignorance of the Scriptures.

These verses begin a longer passage showing how members of Christ's body are to behave in their social relationships. We read of husbands and wives, of parents and children, of masters and slaves. The passage follows naturally Paul's statement in verse 21 that Christians should submit to one another.

We should be careful, however, not to confuse the principle of submission as it is presented in verse 21 with that which follows. In verse 21 Paul calls for submission on a personal level, the subjection of all Christians to all other Christians as servants to one another. Submission on a social level is something different, for it is related to the principle of authority, which governs all human relationships. All of us live in a double relationship to others: a personal relationship in which we can humbly accept wrongs and submit to injustice, and a social relationship in which we must maintain the lines of authority which come from God. Wise is the man who can distinguish clearly between the two.

I. WIVES AND SUBMISSION (5:22-24)

Few passages are more contested or misunderstood than this. In spite of our emotional reaction to these seemingly harsh words, however, let us understand one thing very clearly: this is God's pattern for the marriage relationship. We must not explain away the Word of God by saying that these statements only reflect Paul's personal prejudice or that they are culturally out of date.

"Wives, submit yourselves." Just what does this mean? Of course, it does not mean that the wife is to become the slave of the husband. The whole tenor of this beautiful passage contradicts such an interpretation. The wife is the husband's equal, taken from his side. Marriage, as it is intended by God, is teamwork destined to bring complete fulfillment to both members. In every team there must be a leader; in marriage, the leader is to be the husband.

1. Submission is voluntary. Verb tenses are always important; Paul does not say, "Wives, be submissive," but rather, "Wives, submit." Anyone willing to think about this for a few minutes will see that submission, rather than suppressing the wife's freedom, is actually an active expression of it.

Christian marriage is not imposed by others; the wife, as well as the husband, enters into it freely. Further, once the marriage is consummated, the husband is given no right to impose his authority by force or punishment. Submission must be through the wife's choice. In every situation she can choose to submit, or she can choose not to submit. Submission is God's will, but the wife does not have to obey this command any more than she has to obey any other command in the Word.

In other words, Paul is not saying, "Husbands, force your wives to submit to your authority." The command made to the husband is of an entirely different nature, as we shall see. No, Paul addresses this command to the wife. He places the responsibility squarely on her. And in doing so, rather than destroying her freedom, he appeals to it, seeking to develop it through active obedience.

You see, we must always distinguish between real freedom on the one hand, and independence on the other. To be free is not to be independent. True freedom is to be able to move freely within the boundaries God has traced for our lives, finding fulfillment within the scope of His will. Liberation does not come from destroying those boundaries. A woman is not liberated when she ceases to become a woman, nor a wife when she ceases to accept her high calling. Liberation comes from within and consists of a joyful acceptance of one's mission.

2. "As unto the Lord" (v. 22). Submission to the husband begins to make sense when we see it in its wider context. The Lord ordained marriage and made the ground rules for its success. The appalling divorce rate in the United States is hardly convincing testimony that man can ignore God's rules and find happiness.

The phrase "as unto the Lord" means two things about the wife's relation to her husband. First, it means that once she has accepted marriage, the only way she can submit fully to the Lord is to submit to her husband. God has ordained the principle of authority in all human relationships; His will for our lives conforms to the patterns He has established. "Anyone who rebels against authority is resisting a divine institution" (Rom. 13:2, NEB).

Second, it is *because* the wife submits to the Lord that she can submit to her husband. Human authority is tolerable because there is higher authority to which we can appeal. God never expects us to submit to human authority which violates His laws. To submit to another without doing so "as unto the Lord" could lead to exploitation. Submission as to Him brings freedom, knowing that above all human authority is a God who is on the throne and who allows into our lives only what He wills.

3. "The husband is the head of the wife" (v. 23). Though we cannot understand fully why the man instead of the wife is the head of the marriage, anyone who has even elementary experience in management knows that no organization can have two heads and function properly. Further, the head of an organization is not necessarily expected to be the most intelligent or most capable member. His job is to make the final decisions, then to assume the responsibility for them. Often he makes the wrong decisions, but if there is a spirit of teamwork in the organization, everyone will get behind him and work together.

A wife can submit to her husband and still perform fully as a person. He needs her advice, and if he knows she will allow him to exercise his responsibility as head of the home, he will seek her advice. When good management principles are applied, the head of an organization is not a dictator who uses others to fulfill his personal ambition. It is rather his job to make decisions that will help the entire team to coordinate its gifts for accomplishing the goals that have been agreed upon.

Therefore, marriage is more than joining two bodies to make one flesh; it is joining two heads as well. If the wife need not feel inferior to her husband in the physical union of their bodies, neither should she unwillingly submit her mind to his so that the two can become one.

4. "In everything" (v. 24). Submission is to be active; it is also to be total. Unity of the couple is achieved only through complete sharing. If the wife insists on keeping certain areas of her life autonomous, she deprives these areas of her husband's love.

Some couples, because of a refusal to fuse their wills into one, create a sort of partnership rather than a team. The husband marks off certain areas of responsibility and acts independently in those areas, and the wife does the same. This is not marriage in its total expression. Marriage is more than sharing bodies. It is sharing spirits. Submission must extend to all aspects of marriage in order for fulfillment to be total.

II. HUSBANDS AND LOVE (5:25-27)

Sometimes people react so negatively to the first command that they fail to see the second. Of the two, however, the second is certainly the greater. Through submission the wife has the power to create the unity which makes love operative, but it is love which brings the union to perfection.

"Husbands, love your wives." For the newlywed, such a command seems superfluous; for the husband whose first love has died, it seems unattainable. But in both cases, it is a command which is both necessary and achievable.

Just as the wife is to initiate submission, so the husband is to initiate love. This does not mean, of course, that wives have no obligation to love; it does mean that the responsibility for preserving love rests squarely on the shoulders of the man. When something happens to rupture their spiritual communion, it is he who is to initiate the reconciliation.

1. What love is. We use the word "love" to refer to three kinds of sharing: physical, which is the sharing of bodies; emotional, which is the sharing of feelings; and spiritual, which is sharing on the level of intelligence and will. Though a husband's love for his wife is both physical and emotional, it is important to understand that the love commanded here is the same kind as Christ showed for His Church. It is love which grows out of the will to love, love based on choice.

Spiritual love rises above circumstances and goes beyond personality. Physical love is limited to the body; emotional love is limited to the feelings; but spiritual love has no limits, for God has placed eternity in man's heart. All true love must grow, or else it will perish. Those couples whose love is based only on physical attraction or emotional appeal will someday find boredom creeping into their relationship. Couples whose love grows through the years have learned to cultivate love on the spiritual level. Even suffering cannot quench such love; rather, it provides opportunity for it to deepen.

Because spiritual love grows out of the will to love, this command offers great hope to those whose marriages are in trouble. For God never commands the impossible. Every Christian husband, no matter how far his marriage has deteriorated, can purpose today to begin obeying God, and trust the Holy Spirit to provide the power he lacks. And unless he is willing to obey this command, all the marriage counseling he can get will be worthless. It only takes one to bring love back into the marriage—and that one is to be the husband. Of course, it takes two for this love to find fulfillment; there is no guarantee that a wife will respond to the love her husband offers. But until he is willing to provide it, she has nothing to respond to.

2. What love does (vv. 25-27). How is this command to be obeyed? Just how must the husband express his love? To answer this question Paul points us to the example of Christ's love for the Church and in doing so presents the most beautiful and personal of the three images of the Church found in Ephesians: that of a bride. The Church is Christ's *body*; it is a living and growing organism, exhibiting unity and diversity. The Church is a *building*; it has order and structure and is the dwelling place of God. The Church is a *bride*; it is the object of His love and is destined to be "a glorious church, not having spot, or wrinkle."

Christ's love for the Church. From all eternity, the Church was in Christ's mind and was the object of His love. Without His love the Church would never have come into existence. Without His love it could never be perfected.

a. Through love our Lord gave himself for the Church. Verse 2 of this same chapter pointed out that Christ's love brought Him down to earth and sent Him to the cross as our sacrifice.

b. Through love our Lord sanctified the Church by cleansing it with the water of the Word. To sanctify means to set apart for a purpose. In eternity past the Church was chosen as Christ's unique bride; now He is cleansing it by regenerating and purifying it through His Word.

c. Through love our Lord will present the Church to himself as something glorious. It will be without spot or wrinkle, which means it will be free from defects both within and without. It will be holy and without blemish. The Church is destined to perfection and awaits the bridegroom's coming for this glorious consummation.

The husband's love for his wife. Verses 25 to 27 therefore present a comparison which is simply staggering. They imply that a husband's love for his wife should have basically the same effect upon her as the Lord's love has upon the Church. Of course, Christ's union with the Church is marked by His perfection; no human relationship will ever be "without spot or wrinkle."

Now, let us back up a bit and try to discover, from Christ's example, how husbands should love their wives.

a. Husbands should love their wives by giving themselves to them. In the marriage ceremony all of us who are husbands promised ourselves to our brides until death should sever this union. But the marriage ceremony is only the beginning.

One of the most common complaints of wives is that their husbands have no time for them. To be sure, few husbands fail to give their wives things: they are faithful to provide a home, food, and other material needs. But love is more than giving of what we possess: it is the giving of self. Further, we can measure this gift only by time. The husband who is not spending time with his wife is a husband who is not loving in actual practice, even though he may insist that his wife means everything to him.

Christ's gift to the Church was sacrificial, and in our day any gift of our time will mean sacrificing something else. Time cannot be stretched; we have but a limited supply of it. Much of our time is not our own. But how we use the rest is a good indication of what we love.

b. Husbands should love their wives by sanctifying them. To sanctify means to set apart; wives are to be set apart—from the beginning of our marriage to the end—as the unique objects of their husbands' love. The kind of love God expects men to have for their wives cannot be shared with other women. When we hear the term "wife-swapping," we generally think of it only in sexual terms; there is, however, a great deal of wife-swapping among Christians that does not go that far, but that can only be detrimental to total love in marriage. Flirting with another's mate might seem cute, but it is not; though one's wife might make a joke about it, she is inwardly wounded.

To set apart one's wife, however, is more than negative fidelity. Jesus sanctified the Church by His Word. It is through words that a husband sets apart his chosen one. There can be no true expression of love without verbal communication; for some reason, most couples find communication difficult. Wives want to be spoken to; they also want to be heard. If things are going badly in your marriage, probably the place to begin working is in the area of meaningful conversation.

c. Husbands should love their wives by perfecting them. Through His love, Jesus is creating a glorious Church. Through love, the husband exercises a stupenduous power over his wife—the power of making her something glorious. Perfect wives are not found; they are made. Whatever we emphasize in the lives of our mates will eventually become a part of their character. Just as everyone unconsciously responds to his image of himself, so wives respond to the image created by their husbands. By emphasizing faults, we make them grow; the same is true of good qualities.

Christ's love for the Church consisted of first declaring it perfect (justification), then treating it as such. "Husbands, love your wives, even as Christ also loved the church."

III. ONE FLESH (5:28-33)

Paul has presented two great commands revealing the divine pattern for marriage: love and submission. He has illustrated these by comparing marriage to Christ's union with the Church. Now, to conclude, he goes deeper in this comparison, rooting the commands in the very nature of the marriage relationship and our union with Christ.

1. Marriage constitutes a new body (vv. 28-30). Men ought to love their wives as their own bodies. Usually we take this to mean that just as a man loves his own physical body, so he should love his wife. The meaning, however, seems to be deeper. Paul is commanding men to love their wives, because in the marriage relationship their wives constitute their own bodies. In this sense, he who loves his wife is actually loving his own body.

Just as our union with Christ and with other Christians forms a new spiritual body which is more than a simple association of like-minded people, so marriage creates something new. When a man gives himself to a woman in marriage, something new is created: a new body, in which each member, while retaining his own personality, becomes fused into something bigger than both.

Therefore, this body—the marriage—is to be nourished and cherished. Nourishment must be more than physical, because the body is more than physical. Nothing necessary to feed the marriage and to keep it is to be denied. The word "cherish" means literally to keep warm. Bodies are kept warm by protecting them from cold and maintaining an atmosphere in which they can function comfortably. Marriages are to be protected in the same way.

The phrase "of his flesh, and of his bones," does not appear in the best manuscripts. This passage is to be understood in the spiritual sense.

2. "Two shall be one flesh" (vv. 31-33). Verse 31 is quoted from Genesis 2:24, where marriage was instituted, and from Mark 10:7-8, where divorce is forbidden. Here it is used to show the vital unity which exists in marriage.

Verse 31 is in three parts. First, it states that a man must leave his father and mother. The marriage relationship cancels previous family obligations. It is common knowledge that if both mates do not sever their previous family ties, the marriage will suffer. The act of leaving father and mother must be decisive; for this reason, in every culture, marriage begins with a formal ceremony.

Second, this verse states that a man must join himself to his wife. This is love in its total expression—spiritual, emotional, and physical. It is the complete identification of two human beings in a relationship which is more intimate than any other possible. For two human beings to engage in sexual relationships outside marriage is to make mockery of this deep truth, as Paul points out in I Corinthians 6:16.

Third, this verse states that the two become "one flesh." This is the result of the other two conditions. It means much more than physical union; husband and wife are "one flesh" because their relationship creates a new body, of which the physical union of their bodies is only an expression.

"This is a great mystery." A mystery, as we have seen, is the revelation of a previously hidden truth. Does this phrase apply to marriage or to the Church? The one precedes; the other follows; and it is not easy to know just what Paul refers to. Perhaps the best answer is that it refers to both. Just as the true nature of the Church is a mystery now revealed, the revelation of the Church has in turn revealed truth about marriage which was formerly understood only imperfectly. People have always understood that physical union brought two bodies together; now they are to learn that marriage itself creates a new body in which perfection is to be realized through love and submission.

But whether or not we can fully understand all the implications, we can nevertheless obey the commands. Paul ends his remarkable passage on marriage by reminding us again of the two obligations on which every successful marriage must be grounded. Even though the mystery is great, husbands should not forget to love, or wives to submit.

There is one little change, however, in the final verse. This change is precious. The word "submission" has been changed to "reverence." The submissive wife someday begins to adore the one who loves her.

Questions for Discussion

1. What are areas in your life in which you find it difficult to distinguish between purely personal submission and social submission?

2. What is the difference between liberation, freedom, and independence?

3. Does the wife's submission mean that she cannot make decisions of

her own?

4. Should a wife submit to her husband even when her husband does not love her?

5. How can love which is commanded be real love?

6. How should a husband's love be expressed in a relationship in which his wife takes the leadership?

7. In what way is the marriage relationship a new body?

12

At Home and Work

EPHESIANS 6:1-9

THE CHAPTER OUTLINED:

I. **Children and Parents**
1. "Children, obey your parents"
2. "In the Lord"
3. "Fathers, provoke not your children to wrath"
4. "Bring them up in the nurture and admonition
   of the Lord"

II. **Slaves and Masters**
1. "Servants, be obedient"
2. "And, ye masters"

Anyone who reads his New Testament attentively cannot help but be impressed by its emphasis on social obligations. Though the theme of Ephesians is the Church, the implications of Paul's teaching touch all the Christian's relationships. The Church is Christ's body, but it is still in the world. In addition to belonging to a church, the Christian lives in many other communities: his home, his neighborhood, and the people with whom he works. When he moves from one sphere to another, he must exhibit no conflict in his behavior. He has no right to adopt a double standard.

Not only do the Scriptures stress healthy human relationships; they also tell us how to maintain them. Some Christians tend to see their convictions as a hindrance to freedom at home or at work. Such an opinion must surely be based on a misunderstanding of the nature of Biblical principles. These basic principles are universal, not simply because they are Christian, but because they are inherently right.

Paul in Ephesians 5 dealt with the principle of submission; he stated that the Christian was to submit personally to all, and that wives were to submit to their husbands. He now turns to submission as it applies in the home and at work.

I. CHILDREN AND PARENTS (6:1-4)

Someone has said that it is a parent's task to break his child's will without breaking his spirit. Verses 1 to 4 present essentially this truth. To break a child's will is to teach him to submit to higher authority. To break his spirit would be to destroy his capacity for creativity. Children must have freedom to develop their personalities; their personalities must develop, however, within the limits that God has traced. When fire is kept in a furnace, it will bring warmth to an entire house. When it escapes, it destroys.

Theories of child-rearing swing back and forth like a pendulum between total freedom and unconditional obedience. The poor parent, who has to embark on this the most difficult of all tasks with no previous experience, finds himself at a loss before the choice of methods thrown at him. Mistakes are tragic, and yet he sometimes finds his most trusted counselor, whose writings became the holy writ on child-rearing, admit after years of damage that his ideas were wrong.

Yet, the Scriptures are plain for those who have the courage to apply them. "Children, obey your parents." This implies discipline. "Fathers, do not provoke your children to anger." Discipline is to be administered in love.

1. "Children, obey your parents" (v. 1). When a little bundle of joy arrives in the home of new parents, there begins almost immediately a fierce battle of the wills which increases until either the parent or the child surrenders. Some parents, bitterly, can even remember the circumstances in which their child won the final battle simply because they lost their courage.

Children learn security and responsibility only through obedience. Discipline provides the boundaries within which their personality can develop normally. If they never encounter an unconditional "no," they develop emotional problems. Complexes are the result not of discipline properly administered, but rather of the lack of it.

Most of a child's personality traits are established in the first few years of his life by his relationship with his parents. What, then, can be done when parents wake up after many years of faulty discipline to face the fact that they have failed with their children? Is all lost? Thanks to God, nothing is ever "all lost" when put into His hands. We cannot always correct past mistakes, but it is never too late to begin doing right, even though to impose discipline after years of laxness is difficult. The parent who is convicted of wrongdoing in this area should confess his errors frankly to his children, ask their forgiveness for the harm he has caused them, and announce that a new era has begun.

Though obedience is something that parents must teach their children, this commandment is addressed to the children themselves. As a child grows, discipline depends less on punishment and more on instruction, requiring obedience which comes from his will to obey.

Let us examine more carefully the three main words of the statement of verse 1: "children," "obey," and "parents."

Children. The command to obey is clear enough when a child is small, but as he grows, the matter becomes more complex. When does a child cease to be subject to parental authority? A child of forty, married and established in life, usually does not return to his parents to ask their permission about decisions he has to make. But what about a child of eighteen, or twenty-one, or twenty-five?

Perhaps it is impossible to give an absolute answer to this question, but it would seem that since obedience to parents falls in the category of social obligations, this command cannot be completely divorced from the accepted social practices in a person's environment. In every culture there comes a time when a child is no longer a child. In some cultures this event is marked by elaborate ceremonies. In Western civilizations, in which a child is dependent upon his parents for longer periods of time, adulthood is harder to define. Yet there comes a time when each child must free himself from dependence on his parents and assume responsibility for his actions. At that time he is free to make his own decisions. To be sure, he still goes to his parents for advice; but the parents must no longer expect him to yield to their will if his convictions differ from theirs.

Obey. To obey is to submit to a higher authority. There is much confusion around this word. Obedience does not require agreement. It is not dependent upon complete understanding of the problem. It does not abrogate discussion. It merely means that the person who has to carry ultimate responsibility is the one who has the right to make the ultimate decisions, and that those under his authority must respect this right to help him in his task.

A child's obedience of his parents falls in the larger sphere of the divine principle of authority. Between God and man is a chain of command; God's will for each individual is that he submit to those who are over him. No Christian can pretend to be spiritual if he rejects this principle.

Now, it is important to realize that the home is the place where the principle of authority is to be learned. If a child does not learn obedience at home, he will probably reject authority at school. Later, he will reject responsibility at work and toward the laws of his state. This rejection of authority will prevent his proper functioning in the Church and may even hinder his submission to the Lord Himself. The consequences are grave indeed; refusal of authority is even listed as a sign of the end time.

Parents. This word is plural. Children are to obey both mother and father, indiscriminately. What tragedy when parents are not united on the question of discipline! The harm they can do in a child's life is sometimes irreparable. If there is any area in which parents absolutely *must* agree, it is this. If agreement is impossible, the wife must submit to the husband, and the parents must present a united front for their children. The inner confusion and frustration of a child who can play off one parent against another can result in permanent damage to his personality and inability to function socially.

2. "In the Lord" (vv. 1-3). Parents have the right to impose authority on their children, for this right is given by God, to whom they also owe obedience. Children can trustingly obey their parents, because they are also children of a higher power, who placed them in their particular family for a reason and to whom they can have recourse when things go wrong.

Paul justifies his command by saying simply, "for this is right." Obedience to parents is not just an arbitrary injunction imposed by a Judeo-Christian mentality; it is inherently right because of the very nature of things. The home is the basic unit of human society. A breakdown of the home will lead to a breakdown of society in general, as we in the United States are witnessing to our dismay. We are made in the image of God and placed in God's world. He knows us well enough to dictate proper behavior for our own good.

Because obedience to parents is "right," it is found in the law. "Honour thy father and mother" is one of the Ten Commandments. This is "the first commandment with promise," in that God promises to those who obey it long life and prosperity. For the nation of Israel, God's judgment with its resulting dispersion was the punishment of disregarding the Law. Today, long and prosperous life is being threatened by violence and a refusal of basic human rights. Some would trace this directly to a breakdown in discipline in the home.

3. **"Fathers, provoke not your children to wrath" (v. 4).** "Children, obey your parents" means discipline. "Provoke not your children to wrath" is discipline in love. Good discipline will break the will; bad discipline will break the spirit. In the parallel passage in Colossians Paul adds the phrase, "lest they be discouraged" (Col. 3:21).

How can we discipline our children without provoking them to anger? This subject would take chapters to develop properly, but these three suggestions might avert some deep hurts in your children's lives.

Discipline must be consistent. How can a parent expect his child to learn right and wrong if he does not follow through with his threats? Parents must be cautious in threatening punishment—commands should be limited to what is important—but once the punishment is announced, it must be applied. Too often discipline reflects a parent's mood more than it does the nature of his child's offense. No discipline should be administered in anger; it then is an expression of carnality.

Because parents frequently make mistakes in discipling their children, they must be willing to ask forgiveness. But in doing so they must make it plain that they are sorry not because punishment was administered, but because it was done in the wrong way. When a parent asks his child's forgiveness, the child's respect for him rises considerably.

Discipline must be for disobedience and not for mistakes. What discouragement to a child when he is punished for spilling his milk, but let go for refusing to pick up his toys! Whether or not to discipline should not be determined by whether the offense is big or little. It should always accompany a willful refusal of the parents' orders, even when the offense seems minor. On the other hand, to punish a child for mistakes is to break his spirit and discourage him from taking initiative.

Discipline must be for acts, not for character. To punish a child for lying will teach him the difference between truth and falsehood. To brand him a liar is to make a character judgment which will be damaging to his personality. Children are not harmed when they are punished for wrong acts; however, if parents create for them a negative self-image, they will gradually conform to it.

4. **"Bring them up in the nurture and admonition of the Lord" (v. 4).** "Nurture" is correction; "admonition" is instruction. The first is usually administered with a stick, at least when the children are small. "Withhold not correction from the child: for if thou beatest him with the rod, he shall not die" (Prov. 23:13). Nurture is discipline as it is applied to the body. Admonition is administered by words. It is discipline as it is applied to the mind. According to God's command, both are necessary. Children who have had only reasoning and no discipline will think they should only obey when they are convinced of the rightness of an action. On the other hand, children who have had only the stick and no reasoning will never grow into moral adulthood.

Reasoned instructions will teach the child why some things are right and others are wrong and on what authority we make moral judgments. This instruction will be "of the Lord," for it will consist of principles from the Word of God. The child will learn that his parents are trying to obey the same authority they are imposing on their children.

"All scripture is given by inspiration of God, and is profitable for doctrine, for reproof, for correction, for instruction in righteousness" (II Tim. 3:16). In reasoning with his child, a parent will develop his child's spiritual capacities.

II. SLAVES AND MASTERS (6:5-9)

The word "servant" means "slave." Paul addressses verses 5 to 8 to those who, though freed from bondage of sin and made fellow citizens with the saints, are subject to earthly masters. Slavery was common at the time this letter was written; rather than attack it directly, however, Paul seeks to raise both slave and master to an understanding of their spiritual responsibility. History proves that this is the wisest way to abolish injustice.

We should remember, however, that slavery in the first century did not always carry the same humiliation that we associate with slavery in general. The slave was often the counterpart of today's employee. The admonitions given in these verses apply not only to slaves and masters of the first century, but also to employees and employers in whatever century they live.

1. "Servants, be obedient" (vv. 5-8). We have already discussed the principle of authority in some detail with respect to wives and children. Though in each sphere of human relationship obedience assumes a different form, the principle remains the same. Paul elaborates the principle here with respect to servants by stating *to whom* obedience is due, *how* servants are to obey, and *why* obedience is commanded.

Obedience is due to those who are masters in the flesh. The wife is to obey the husband, because they have become "one flesh." The employee is to obey his employer, because he is his master "in the flesh." In the former case the obedience is to be "in all things." In the latter it is limited and temporary. Obedience "in the flesh" is defined by the nature of the relationship. An employer has no right to dictate to his employee how he should conduct his home or spend his leisure hours. But he does have the right to tell him how his work is to be done.

The right of employers to command their employees is often contested. However, the man who has to assume final responsibility is the man who has the right to give orders. If obedience was expected of slaves in an unjust system, it is certainly no less right from those who benefit from just social conditions.

Obedience is to be "as unto Christ." In three statements Paul associates obedience with the Lord. Verse 5 says, "as unto Christ," verse 6, "as the servants of Christ," and verse 7, "as to the Lord." Unless employees obey from the heart, rules and regulations imposed by their employers only produce outward conformity.

In these verses Paul makes three statements as to how employees are to obey.

a. "With fear and trembling, in singleness of your heart." The fear and trembling are not of the employer, but rather Christ, and indicate the reverence and devotion with which we should serve. The same expression is used in I Corinthians 2:3, where Paul speaks of his ministry, and in II Corinthians 7:15, where he speaks of the obedience of Christians. "Singleness of heart" indicates purpose, the determination to carry through with orders in spite of the temptation to be led astray by conflicting desires.

b. "Not with eye-service, as menpleasers; but . . . from the heart." Some workers perform only when they are being watched. If the foreman is near, they are hard at it; when he walks off, production decreases considerably. Others do their tasks not from a sense of duty, but because they want to curry favor·with their superiors, hoping for advancement or higher wages.

c. "Doing service, as to the Lord." Work, whether it is performed by a slave for his master or by a worker for his employer, is to be considered primarily as service. Whether bond or free, we are all the servants of our Lord. Unfortunately, industrialization has destroyed the real meaning of work; rather than being of means of serving, it is only a means of making money. This explains more than anything else the deterioration we see in the quality of production and the discontent of workers. The philosophy of the worker has become to work the least possible to make the most money. It is a pity that many do not understand that happiness in work does not come from getting more and more, but from increased giving of themselves.

Paul calls work "doing the will of God." When an employer gives us a task to do, that task becomes God's will for our lives. We can do it therefore with "good will," realizing that we are doing it primarily for Him.

Obedience brings its reward. Verse 8 states a truth that is applicable in working circles today. In Paul's day slaves worked without pay; today many employees are underpaid. But the final accounting has not yet been made. If a worker sees his job as a means of service for the Lord, he can be certain that God sees the good things he does and will reward him.

Paul raises work to a place of dignity and gives it meaning, no matter how degrading it might seem. He gives work a new dimension entirely, for he makes Christ its object. Just as Jesus rebuked the disciples for accusing Mary of wasting her expensive ointment by pouring it out on Him, so He would rebuke us for thinking our lives are wasted if we give them to Him, in whatever capacity we are working. To serve others can also be to serve

Christ.

On the other hand, these verses should be unsettling to Christian employees who see their work only as a means of getting a pay check. How easy it is for the Christian to adopt the mentality of the world, trying to get the most while giving the least.

2. "And, ye masters" (v. 9). Paul's exhortations are not limited to the servants; he terminates his passage on human relationships by turning to the masters, reminding them strongly that they too have a Master who is in heaven, and that there is no respect of persons with Him.

The command addressed to masters is in two parts. First, it is to "do the same things unto them," referring them to the exhortations he has already directed to the servants. This command does not mean, of course, that the employers are to obey their workers; that would be a violation of the principle Paul is teaching. It does mean, however, that even masters should see themselves as servants. On the social level, employers have authority over their employees; on a personal level, all are servants of one another.

In other words, the Christian should see his work as a means of serving others, whether he is in a position of authority or submission. Wise employers use their positions not to exploit their workers, but to provide work as a means of serving the entire community.

The second command is to refrain from threatening. This indicates that masters are to look on their slaves as equals and treat them with dignity. Vile and degrading language, so common among people in authority, is to have no place among Christian employers. The master can exercise the same kind of faith as the servant; when things at work go wrong, he can learn to trust it to the Lord and not browbeat those who are under him.

Thus ends the passage on social relationships. For those in tune with present-day thinking, Paul's words seem strange and outdated. The Christian who has the courage to apply them—whether in the marital relationship, with his children, or at work—will find himself at odds with many of his companions. But these are more than the words of a zealous preacher who lived in a culture entirely foreign to ours. They are the Word of God, and His blessing is promised to those who keep them.

Questions for Discussion

1. Is it really possible to break a child's will without breaking his spirit?
2. How can a parent know when to punish and when not to?
3. What should parents do if they are not in agreement about child

discipline?

4. How does some discipline "provoke a child to wrath"?

5. Is participation in a labor union compatible with Paul's exhortations to servants?

6. To what extent should Christians militate for social justice?

13

Spiritual Warfare

EPHESIANS 6:10-24

THE CHAPTER OUTLINED:

I. The Real Battle
   1. Spiritual conflict requires supernatural power
   2. We stand against the wiles of the devil
   3. We wrestle against invisible powers

II. The Armor of God
   1. The belt of truth
   2. The breastplate of righteousness
   3. Feet shod with readiness
   4. The shield of faith
   5. The helmet of salvation
   6. The sword of the Spirit

III. Praying Always
   1. Prayer and the unseen world
   2. "Praying always"
   3. "That . . . I may speak boldly"

Paul's letter to the Ephesians begins with a magnificent hymn of praise to God the Father, Son, and Spirit, in which God's eternal plan is revealed: to unite all things in Christ. Christ has been exalted above all other authority and been made the head of the Church, which is His body. The Church is a mystery, hidden in ages past, but now revealed, composed of those who have been saved by God's grace and brought together into one spiritual family, in which the barriers between Jew and Gentile have been abolished.

After laying a doctrinal foundation for the Church, the letter then tells how its members are to walk. They are to preserve its unity, based on its uniqueness and realized by the diversity of its ministry. Their walk must contrast with that of the pagans; they should not grieve the Spirit by carnal conduct, but on the contrary be filled with Him by walking in love, light, and wisdom. This walk must express itself in healthy social relationships in the home and at work, where the principle of authority must be respected.

Now, to complete its teaching, the Ephesian letter lifts the veil from the unseen world and reveals how Christians are to conduct themselves in their conflict with spiritual enemies. It is natural that this section should follow directly the passages on human relationships. Whenever people are with people—whether in the church, society, the home, or work—conflicts arise. These conflicts bring Christians into opposition, destroying the unity necessary for the Church's edification and perfection. Paul wants us to see that though becoming a Christian does not end conflict, conflict should be seen on a higher level than man against man. "We wrestle not against flesh and blood, but against principalities."

I. THE REAL BATTLE (6:10-12)

In many wars battles are fought on the wrong fronts. God's children have no business wasting their energies fighting one another. The real battle is in a different sphere: it is against the forces of the invisible world.

1. Spiritual conflict requires supernatural power (v. 10). In Ephesians 1:19 Paul used four different terms to describe the power that raised Christ from the dead and set Him above all other authority. Three of those terms are repeated here to describe the power we need for our spiritual warfare. These terms teach us that God's power is inherent in His nature, expressed in His acts, and transmissible to His servants.

The command in verse 10 is to "be empowered." The Christian can receive power, but he cannot generate it. In spiritual warfare, the human powers of physical strength, emotional appeal, and logical persuasion are useless. Our enemy is spiritual; so must be our power.

2. We stand against the wiles of the devil (v. 11). Some people see the devil everywhere; others do not even accept his existence. Neither of these extremes represents Biblical teaching. The spiritual forces against whom we must battle form an unholy hierarchy, with Satan at the top, ruling over a seemingly organized system of princes, authorities, rulers, and powers who are able to influence the events of the visible world.

Many Christians blame the devil for things he is innocent of. Most of our problems come from our sinful nature, and it is active enough not to need constant diabolical prodding. Further, it is extremely doubtful that any of us have had personal dealings with the devil. Our Lord is omnipotent, so that even the most insignificant Christian can know Him personally. The prince of darkness, however, must work through his countless subordinates, and only rarely intervenes directly in the affairs of men, as he did with Job. The great exception will be in the end times, when it seems evident that the Antichrist will be a man personally indwelt by Satan, just as demoniacs are possessed by Satan's subordinates.

But though we may never face the devil personally, we must stand firm against his wiles. The word translated "wiles" is the Greek word from which we get our term "methods." Just as God has a strategy, so does Satan. God's plan is to submit all things to Christ; Satan's is to submit them to himself. To be able to fulfill God's plan, we must be able to stand against Satan's.

3. We wrestle against invisible powers (v. 12). Wrestling is hard enough when we can see our adversary; ours is hidden behind a veil of darkness. Although few Christians have probably ever wrestled against the devil himself, all Christians are engaged in conflict with his spiritual subordinates. If our eyes could be opened to the invisible world, we would probably be staggered at the amount of spiritual activity going on around us.

In verse 12 Paul uses four terms to designate these unseen powers—terms which could refer to four orders in the satanic hierarchy, though this is only a supposition. The first, "principalities," would certainly be the highest order, perhaps corresponding to one of God's archangels, Michael, who was inferior in order to Satan (Jude 9). The second, "powers" or "authorities," could be those who are given jurisdiction over whole areas of Satan's strategy. The third, "rulers of the darkness of this world," must refer to the "world rulers" such as Daniel encountered in the mysterious "prince of Persia" (Dan. 10:13), who was doubtless the invisible counterpart to the visible ruler. The fourth, "spiritual wickedness," should be translated "spiritual powers of wickedness" and perhaps refers to the subordinate messengers charged with carrying out the orders of their superiors.

It seems significant that Paul should follow his passage about submission to authority with this one about our spiritual conflict. Between the Christian and God there is a chain of authority. Satan's strategy is to usurp God's authority and put it under his own. To reject God's authority, even in the person of a husband, parent, or employer, is to risk exposing ourselves to Satan's (see, for example I Cor. 11:10).

II. THE ARMOR OF GOD (6:13-17)

Verses 13 to 17 constitute one of the great passages of the New Testament, the theme of thousands of sermons and studies. Writing as a prisoner in Rome, Paul is well acquainted with the battle dress of Roman soldiers and uses it as an illustration of the Christian's spiritual armor.

Christians are to "withstand in the evil day, and having done all, to stand." The evil day is not necessarily the end times, when Satan's power will be unleashed in its fullness; in this verse it refers to any day of crisis in the life of the child of God. Since our enemy is invisible, we do not know when he is going to attack; the evil day could be today, or tomorrow. Because his attacks usually come unexpectedly, the Christian must be spiritually ready to meet them. It is too late to put on the armor after the battle starts. If we want to withstand in the evil day, we must clothe ourselves with God's power before that day comes.

It is important for us to learn one thing: God's power is associated with God's armor. To "be strong in the Lord, and in the power of his might," we must "put on the whole armour of God." Many Christians are seeking power, but are neglecting the armor.

1. The belt of truth (v. 14). The belt was a leather girdle worn over the tunic to support the breastplate and scabbard. It was the first part of the armor to be put on.

When Paul said to put off the old man and put on the new, his first command was, "Wherefore putting away lying, speak every man truth with his neighbour: for we are members one of another" (4:25). Members of Christ's body are to speak "the truth in love" (4:15). The belt is the part of the armor which holds the rest in place. Without truth we are impotent before our spiritual enemies, for Satan is the father of lies, and to engage in lying is to place ourselves squarely under his authority.

Putting on truth, however, means much more than abstaining from lying. It is to see ourselves as we really are, sacrificing the facade that we all love to hide behind. Most people try to project an inaccurate image of themselves. But, remember, a person's true self is easily discerned by others. Truth has a way of showing through, and Paul admonishes the Christian to put on truth.

Jesus is the truth. We can become true because He is true. Truth cannot be generated by man; its source is Christ, the Creator of all things visible and invisible.

2. The breastplate of righteousness (v. 14). The breastplate was the part of the soldier's armor which was attached to the belt and which protected the vital organs.

In reading these words our first question is, "Whose righteousness—His or ours?" Certainly, it is first and foremost His. The Christian is never expected to stand up in his own righteousness against Satan. We must be justified—clothed in the righteousness of Christ.

How does the breastplate of righteousness defeat Satan's strategy? It allows us to accept ourselves and others on the basis of Christ's goodness, and not our own. The Church is built on the reconciliation our Lord achieved by His death and resurrection. We accept men because Christ has accepted them. If we accept them on this basis, even Satan cannot drive a wedge between us.

Of course, putting on the breastplate of righteousness means more than simply standing in the righteousness of Christ; it means also reflecting His righteousness in our conduct. If honesty is transparency, righteousness is consistency. Being righteous is being fair in our dealings with others.

In declaring us righteous, our Lord frankly forgives us of our sins. To put on righteousness requires forgiving others as well. "To whom ye forgive any thing, I forgive also: for if I forgave any thing, to whom I forgave it, for your sakes forgave I it in the person of Christ; lest Satan should get an advantage of us: for we are not ignorant of his devices" (II Cor. 2:10-11).

3. Feet shod with readiness (v. 15). Proper footwear is one of the most important parts of the warrior's attire. Sometimes the battle is long; the Christian's feet must be properly shod. Paul doubtless alludes here to

Isaiah 52:7: "How beautiful upon the mountains are the feet of him that bringeth good tidings, that publisheth peace."

Once a man has truly met the Lord, he usually has no trouble knowing what the Gospel is. But how many Christians are ready to share the Gospel? It is no accident that this part of the armor concerns the feet. Readiness to share produces willingness to go to those who are in need.

It is only through the Gospel that men can be wrenched from Satan's authority and put under the authority of Christ. Further, it is only through readiness to share the Gospel that the Christian finds himself fully under the Master's authority. "All authority is given unto me in heaven and in earth," proclaimed Christ. "Go ye therefore" (Matt. 28:18-19).

It is no contradiction of terms to read that we wrestle against our foe with the gospel "of peace." When men are at peace with God, they can be at peace with one another, presenting a united front against their common enemy.

4. The shield of faith (v. 16). "Fiery darts" were arrows dipped in burning pitch before being shot. The shield was a large leather-covered buckler with which the soldier protected himself from these arrows.

Our shield is not just "faith"; it is "the faith." Paul has stated that there is "one faith," which is the message of the death and resurrection of Christ and the spiritual realities it brings to those who accept Him. To take up the shield of faith is to look back to those great events and assure ourselves that "we have not followed cunningly devised fables" (II Peter 1:16), and that our belief is not merely psychological, but that we are truly God's children, born into His family and seated with Him in heavenly places.

In the heat of a spiritual battle Satan resorts to fiery darts of doubt. When doubts come, we must trust something more than our inner feelings; just as the shield does not touch the body but has to be picked up and held, so the Christian's faith is more than his experience of Christ: it is the truth of God's Word.

5. The helmet of salvation (v. 17). A soldier's helmet protects the most important part of his body. Here Paul alludes to Isaiah 59:17, in which God himself is pictured as wearing this helmet.

In I Thessalonians 5:8 Paul states that the helmet is the "hope of salvation." Salvation is not only forgiveness of sins; it is also the assurance that we are to be presented to Christ "a glorious church, not having spot, or wrinkle." We are saved through hope, which is an unwavering confidence that "whom he did foreknow . . . them he also glorified" (Rom.

8:29-30). Therefore, we can be assured that "all things work together for good to them that love God, to them who are the called according to his purpose" (Rom. 8:28).

Most Christians are willing to apply Romans 8:28 when they go to the hospital, but how many claim the same hope when conflicts bring contention into the church? Yet, to be clothed with the helmet of salvation is to believe that in this battle everything is going to turn out as it should. Faith looks to the past and sees that we are all brothers in Christ; hope looks to the future and learns that we are all destined for the same perfection.

6. The sword of the Spirit (v. 17). Most of the armor listed here is for protection. The shoes and the sword, on the other hand, imply that the Christian is to advance into Satan's kingdom and attack. Shoes illustrate readiness to share the Gospel; the sword of the Spirit is God's Word.

The effectiveness of this weapon has been proved by our Lord, in that three times He defeated Satan personally by appealing to it. Satan tried to counter with the same weapon, as he does today, but failed.

If the Christian is to be skilled in anything, it is to be in using God's Word. Using the sword of the Spirit is more than throwing Bible verses at our opponents. We are not wrestling against flesh and blood, but against spiritual powers, which means that the Word of God must pierce "even to the dividing asunder of soul and spirit, and of the joints and marrow," in order to be "a discerner of the thoughts and intents of the heart" (Heb. 4:12). God's Word is to be used not to win arguments, but to win hearts.

III. PRAYING ALWAYS (6:18-20)

Some would make prayer a part of the armor; it would seem more logical to see it as the force making the armor effective. Prayer is so closely bound to all Christian experience that nothing can function without it.

1. Prayer and the unseen world. We tend to see prayer only in two dimensions, the human and the divine. In this passage Paul adds a third, the invisible spirit world. This invisible world is just as real as ours, even though it is hidden from our sight. If God respects the realities of the visible world, He does the same with the world of spirits.

Seeing our conflict as a spiritual battle will awaken our understanding to the tremendous influence that this spiritual world plays in our lives, and that prayer releases a force directly into this third world. It is altogether possible that every earnest prayer triggers a spiritual combat in the heavenlies, and that if we do not see answers to our prayers immediately, it is because that combat is real. Why pray? Because our battle is against more than flesh and blood.

2. **"Praying always" (v. 18).** Nowhere else is the necessity for prayer presented in such all-encompassing terms. Note the repetition of the word "all." We are to pray at all times, with all prayer and supplication, in all perseverance, for all saints.

Prayer is to be at all times—on the good days as well as the evil ones. To pray at all times does not mean the Christian can pray without stopping, but that in any circumstance he can and should seek communication with God.

We are to pray in the Spirit. Our enemy is invisible to us, but not to God. No alien strategy is hidden from His sight. When "we know not what we should pray for as we ought," the Holy Spirit "maketh intercession for us" (Rom. 8:26).

We are to pray with watchfulness. This indicates awareness of what is going on, so that our prayers will not be cut off from reality. Prayer without content is not effective.

3. **"That . . . I may speak boldly" (vv. 19-20).** Paul's prayers reveal some of the reasons for his spiritual greatness. The same is true of his prayer requests. This great man who once exclaimed, "Woe is unto me, if I preach not the gospel!" (I Cor. 9:16), has one final exhortation to make to his beloved friends at Ephesus, and it is a touching revelation of his heart. Would not we request prayer for release from prison were we in similar circumstances? Not Paul. He asks the Ephesian Christians to pray that he will have "utterance."

The prison fetters had not dimmed his vision of his true position. Paul knew he was an ambassador, though presently "in chains." As God's ambassador he had no right to question his Master about his place of service. His concern was faithfully to represent his King by making known the "mystery of the gospel" to those who had yet to understand.

In making this request Paul was perhaps thinking of his coming appearance before the tribunal, where he would share God's message with the highest officials of the empire. Paul's concern was not that he would be released, but that he would speak boldly. He knew he was a chosen vessel, called to bear God's name before kings (Acts 9:15).

These final verses are magnificent! The Apostle's revelations of the Church and his ability to allow his thoughts to soar into the heavenly places with Christ had not blinded him to the work that was yet to be done. May it be the same with us.

In our studies of the Ephesian letter we have been privileged to contemplate "that glorious church." In doing so we have certainly seen the petty problems of our local congregation in a new perspective; perhaps our vision of the Church as the body and bride of Christ has even caused some of these problems to disappear.

Our vision of the Church must not dull our vision of the world, however. Each of us, as Paul, is an ambassador for Him from whom the Church receives its life. He is building His church, and the gates of hades shall not prevail against it—but it is not yet complete. For to many of our friends, the Gospel is still a mystery. May we, at the conclusion of these studies, prepare ourselves anew to share the good news. May God give us the same boldness for which Paul prayed.

Though the beginning of Paul's letter is conventional in its form, the ending is more personal. Verses 21 to 24 present a brief recommendation of Tychicus, followed by a benediction.

Tychicus was one of Paul's most trusted co-workers and was charged not only with the delivery of his letters to the Ephesians, Colossians, and Philemon, but also with the responsibility of giving the Christians a first-hand account of the Apostle's situation at Rome.

Paul's concluding benediction adds a word which was not found in his salutation. In addition to wishing his readers grace and peace (here found in reverse order), he mentions "love with faith." Grace is what God offers; peace is the result of this wonderful gift; love is our response.

Questions for Discussion

1. What is Satan's primary task with respect to the Christian?

2. Can undue preoccupation with Satan actually fit into his strategy?

3. Is there a difference between possession and influence, with respect to demonic activity? Can a true Christian be demon-possessed?

4. What is the relationship of the various parts of the Christian's armor to Satan's strategy?

5. How does understanding of the unseen world add a new dimension to our conception of prayer?

6. Why does Paul so closely associate prayer with preaching the Gospel?

Bibliography

Arndt, William F. and Gingrich, F. Wilbur. *A Greek-English Lexicon of the New Testament*. Chicago: University of Chicago, 1957.

Blaikie, W. G. "Ephesians." In the *Pulpit Commentary*. New York: Funk & Wagnalls.

Bruce, F. F. *The Epistle to the Ephesians*. Westwood, N.J.: Revell, 1961.

Horton, Frank. *L'Epître aux Ephésians*. St.-Légier, Switzerland: Editions Emmaüs.

Kent, Jr., Homer A. *Ephesians*. Chicago: Moody Press, 1971.

Lenski, R. C. H. *The Interpretation of St. Paul's Epistles to the Galatians, to the Ephesians, and to the Philippians*. Columbus: Wartburg, 1937.

Martin, W. G. M. "The Epistle to the Ephesians." In *The New Bible Commentary*. Grand Rapids: Eerdmans, 1954.